Six Who Came
To Serve

TOM CANTLON

Tom Cantlon is also the author of

"Selected Columns, 2001 - 2006"

due out in December of 2011.

CONTENTS

PREFACE

In about the year 2005, as the six people profiled in this book realized their group was entering retirement years, they decided to have a photograph of them taken for the fun of it. That led to the photograph that's on the cover. Jean Phillips, who had been involved in several of their stories and active in community work in Prescott, suggested their stories should be written. That idea languished until it was revived by the author and resulted in this book.

The following accounts of their childhoods, and college days, and early careers, and how they operated their agencies, come from interviews with each of them. Interviews in which they were free to focus on what parts of their story they wanted to convey, what influenced them, what is memorable to them. Interviews in which the personality of each was given free space to come through. For instance the extent to which each wanted to focus on the importance of their childhood varied, with Kathy and Brad particularly having stories of how their upbringing laid the foundation for their later work. Some are more outspoken, well suited to their roles promoting their organizations in the community.

Their stories are woven together in time to follow the story as a group, as they progressed through their stages over the thirty plus years of parallel careers.

There are many other people who were involved in social services over these years and some are mentioned here. Other important people were members of the community who played substantial support roles, and some of them are mentioned too. No doubt some have been inadvertently forgotten, and the contributions of others involved in similar efforts are simply beyond the scope of this book. The connections that start from here and spread like a web to a list of related efforts by the many people actively engaged in the Prescott community could fill numerous other books, and offer a rich vein for other local historians to document.

INTRODUCTION

In 1973 Max Bell moved to Prescott, Arizona to become the one-man "Welfare Department", what later became Child Protective Services. He moved to Prescott after having grown up in nearby towns and going to college in Phoenix. Within six months Gordon Glau, who grew up in Prescott, took a job with the Juvenile Probation Department. A year later Kathleen Murphy went to her first meeting of the board of what would become Big Brothers/Big Sisters. Don Ostendorf moved here to be part of West Yavapai Guidance Clinic, and John Allen came to be part of Catholic Social Services. In 1976 Brad Newman came to head up Yavapai Exceptional Industries.

In a very short time they were each running growing agencies in a growing city. Over the next 30 years and more they led their agencies, guided them through stages of growth, worked together, worked with other members of the community, and improved the lives of many thousands of people.

The end result is thirty plus years of Prescott being a better place. Of organizations that sometimes could have been in competition with one another, instead cooperating. Of not letting bureaucracy get in the way of just getting together with one another, and with other members of the community, spelling out what problems they saw, how they could work together to address them, and being effective at it. Thirty years of young people growing up in broken homes or having mental or drug problems and being guided into becoming happier, more productive members of the community, and all the benefit that comes with that. Of young people starting to get into trouble and being guided out of it, and all the costs and problems they would otherwise have created, being avoided. Of people with handicaps living exceptionally productive and full lives. Thirty years of innovation and leadership, often leading the state and sometimes the nation in their methods and effectiveness. They set out to make a contribution, and they achieved that to an amazing degree in the lives of an enormous number of people in the Prescott community.

Their stories weave together. Some grew up in Arizona, even knowing one another. Others came from across the country. Their stories and how they ran their agencies show their varied personalities and also some commonalities. Their solid backgrounds and the time in which they grew up had profound effects. The Vietnam war had an important, if indirect, effect.

Part of the commonality is in how they approached their young lives. They did not see themselves as simply drone bees in society and just figure on getting whatever job they could, put in their years, and retire. They were down to Earth enough that they did not start off to be rock stars or movie stars, to only later settle into careers. They didn't have the self-centered ambition that leads some people to just focus on the money and shoot for making their first million by thirty. Down to Earth, but with a high enough sense of purpose to be sure they could play some role in making a difference. Having a sense of both the responsibility and the desire of it. Products of the 60s enough to want to see the world become better, and want to be part of that change, and confident they would be a part of that change, but their choice was not to do that by becoming back-to-the-land hippies, or hoping for revolution or a new age. They set out to affect their part of the change in very traditional ways; go to college, gain a skill, start a career, and work day in, day out, for decades, not in world-changing or far reaching ways, but on a more human scale, directly helping the lives of as many people as they could within their time and within the personal reach of themselves and the organizations they ran.

It is also the story of Prescott. These six could not have succeeded if not for tremendous support. Not just monetarily, but with great investments of time and talent. The stories are full of involved members of the community who saw needs in a growing town and addressed them. Later this took the form of working with these organizations. Early on it sometimes took the form of local people seeing a need and no solution at the time, and starting one. What became Big Brothers/Big Sisters, and West Yavapai Guidance Clinic, were started by locals who saw the need for these services, started small, and sought ways to fill those needs.

Looking back, one thing that is clear is that these core, active members of the community had the foresight to see the need for social services in a growing community. That they wanted those who were suffering or disturbed to have help. That their young who start to go wayward be helped back onto solid paths. That a place be made for those less able among them, to be contributing parts of the community too. They wanted the members of their community who needed these services to have them, and they saw that the community would benefit for it.

It is not just the story of these six opening the eyes of a sleepy community. It is not just the story of a community that knew exactly what its needs were and how to fill them and hired people to do it. It was the serendipity of a community that had some idea of the need for such services, open to and willing to support efforts, and six talented, trained, skilled, hard working people who could lead them to exceptional solutions.

All six had good, solid childhoods. So we start there.

Kathleen Murphy

Brad Newman (by Clayton Smith)

Max Bell

Gordon Glau

Don Ostendorf

John Allen

CHILDHOOD

Don

Don Ostendorf, born in 1945, grew up in the very small farm town of Addieville in South Western Illinois. There were 300 people in the town. Going into "town" meant going into Okawville, a bigger town about five miles away. It wasn't very big either, about 1,500 people. About 40 mile further west, and across the river, is St. Louis. His home town still has about 300 people. A town he is very proud of. Most families had farms and most people expected to grow up and continue the farming. As a typical kid there he never went to Chicago until he was an adult. His family or others from the town might travel to St. Louis once in a great while to go to the zoo or a ballgame. As he puts it, "We had each other, and that was okay."

Kathy

Kathy Murphy was born Mary Kathleen Alvey in Phoenix in 1949. She went by "Kathy" in her youth, started using "Kathleen" for work when she started her career, and still goes by "Kathy" to friends.

Phoenix was a much smaller city. There were still some dirt roads, and she would sometimes ride the donkey her parents got for her down Central Avenue. There was no air-conditioning, though she doesn't remember it being as hot as it is now. Some of that "heat island" effect of a big city with a lot of pavement has made what was a hot place even hotter.

She was very close to her father and remembers as a young girl spending many evenings sitting on his lap pestering him while he tried to read.

Other clear memories come from the vacations she and her parents would take. Her father was an avid fisherman and hunter and would take a two-week vacation each year to go fishing, and another to go hunting. She was the youngest child and 7 years younger than her next sibling, so on the fishing trips it was mostly just her and her parents, camping for the two weeks.

Her father would spend his day-time quietly sitting on a river bank, fishing. Kathy suspects that if she were tested she would be found to tend toward Attention Deficit Disorder (ADD), and has been that way since she was a child. While she is not hyperactive, she is energetic, often restless, and not given to sitting quietly and concentrating on one thing. Like fishing. So she would go wandering off, far up and down whatever stream they were on, on a quest for the perfect swimming hole, and enjoying along the way every funny bug, every pretty leaf, every songbird she encountered. In the course of this she gained an unwavering comfort with the outdoors. To this day she says her favorite thing is to be outside.

Both she and her father loved dogs and would always have a very close "pal" that would accompany them on these trips, and who would accompany Kathy in her wanderings.

Over these years she learned of her father's background. He started life in Indiana. At the age of 14, with older parents and the family simply unable to support him, and having a brother he'd never met on a ranch in South Dakota, he was sent off to work with the brother. That began his time as a cowboy, riding with a crew herding cattle from where they were raised to the slaughterhouse. Sometimes driving them hundreds of miles to where they would be loaded on train cars, which he also rode, with the cattle, to cities including Chicago.

He married Kathy's mother and they lived first in Arkansas, then Texas. Since he was a good mechanic he ended up souping up cars and running moonshine. In Texas they were soon smack in the middle of The Great Depression. They lost what they had and moved to Arizona. There they had three girls and and a second boy. Her father had a gas station and mechanic's shop; the Richfield station at 16th Street and Camelback Road. He later opened his own garage, the South Central Garage. He also built race cars for some of the best drivers of the time.

Her mother's influence comes primarily through her home life. They did not have much money, but they ended up in a modest house in what came to be a high end neighborhood in Phoenix. Her mother taught her fine manners and how to get along with all sorts of people, and she always felt she fit right in even though most of her neighbors were better off.

Her mother also sewed a great deal and taught Kathy to do so at an early age. A birthday gift might consist of going shopping at a high end store and then going home with new material that her mom would then construct to look like the ones in the store with whatever modifications desired. Kathy would help her mother with the design and sewing, which she loved doing.

Her father later died when she was a young adult of lung cancer. The lesson that Kathy takes from her father is that he did what he wanted and never worried about what other thought. He never had much money, but he did work at things that suited him. Together with his wife they provided the family a modest but good home and upbringing. While accomplishing those things he set his priority on enjoying life the way he liked to, with lots of time spent wandering around the wilderness, enjoying the outdoors. That's what he wanted to do, and he did it.

Her mother, at the age of 51, with Kathy now in school, re-invented herself. She got her high school equivalency degree, became a court reporter, and lost some weight. Again, the lesson she took from her mother was that you could go after what you wanted to be, and accomplish it. Not in the sense of making huge amounts of money, or fame. Such things weren't valued much in her home to even be sought after. But you could be in control of your life, choose what you wanted to be and how you wanted to live, and achieve it. It ingrained in her the idea that hard steady work could gradually build up to big accomplishments.

During her early school years Kathy developed several strands of thought that wove together to shape her early sense of social structure and social need. She knew her family, though not poor, were low income workers, but she never felt in need. She learned the distinction between those who were poor but didn't act it, and those who were poor and seemed feel or act poor. At the same time she became aware that there were others in her own town of Phoenix and around the world who were disadvantaged or truly in need.

When she was in 4th grade she would go with her older sister to South Phoenix, to some of the poorer, Hispanic Catholic parishes to teach catechism. Seeing the poorer conditions in these schools she was puzzled that, despite they all being Catholic, why their schools were in worse shape and had fewer supplies.

She had some sense of what it meant that her family were low-income workers because many of her friends and school mates came from families that were better off. That was never an issue for her though. She never felt disadvantaged. Part of the reason for that came from her experience with her extended family.

She had many cousins in the area and many North in the Verde Valley. Some of the nearby cousins came from families like hers that were low income workers but who seemed to take care of themselves and whom she didn't think of as poor. Others had parents who were alcoholic and their homes and their children were always dirty and disheveled. She can remember houses where she would never feel comfortable taking her shoes off because the floors were so dirty (this despite the fact she spent most of her young summers barefoot outside) and where the houses smelled and the sheets were stained and dirty.

In later grade school she spent summers with these families while the parents were away at work or just gone. The conditions bothered her so much that she began a program of getting the kids to join her in cleaning up the house. She did what she could in her time with them to instill some sense of power over their situation and control.

Her parents had instilled that sense of pride in her by example. Her father, despite growing up poor had a type of dignity about himself that showed in little ways like being very non-judgmental and fair, and never speaking poorly about others. Her mother was also from a poor household but as Kathy says, "she was raised well." Her mother kept their house clean and their clothes nice, even if it meant doing a great deal of that sewing. More importantly she gave them a sense of the value of intelligence and culture, taught them manners, and gave them a sense of dignity and self worth that allowed her to never have any sense of inferiority when rubbing elbows with much better-off families.

This sense of pride and self worth that she saw in her parents flowed together in her mind with the idea of having some control over ones self, over one's life. In Kathy's mind this pride and this sense of control of one's life equate. Someone who has pride in themselves will feel in control of their life and able to rise out of adverse circumstances. That characteristic later played an important role in her career. She would later come to see that mentoring programs, like Big Brothers/Big Sisters, do just that, help kids who are in circumstances that might rob them of that sense of pride and self control, and helps them to discover that insight. With that added to their quiver they are better able to steer themselves away from trouble and to a better end.

Combined in her then was a lack of any sense of being disadvantaged on her own part, with a clear awareness that there were those who genuinely are disadvantaged. Besides her experiences with her cousins and other parishes in Phoenix, her grade school played some role. The school seemed to be constantly collecting for starving children around the world, for missions to poor children by Catholic nuns of the Mary Knoll order. She jokes that selling candy door to door for such causes was her first experience with fund raising.

Max

Max was born in Iowa in 1949. His family moved to Arizona when he was two. He grew up in Clarkdale and Jerome.

Let's get the lay of the land. There's a ridge of mountains that runs North and South in mid-Arizona, the central feature of which is Mingus Mountain. On either side are towns in our story. On the West side, about a half hour drive West of where the mountain slopes down to the flats is Prescott, at about 5000 feet elevation. There are some other mountains nearby and some rocky dells, the remnants of volcanic activity long ago, and hills with pines, but Mingus is the highest nearby feature. From Prescott's higher hills to its lower areas you can find pine trees and cactus, sometimes together. Some areas you would be lost in forest, and others looking across wide open grass plains.

An old road winds up over Mingus Mountain up to about 7000 feet. At the top of the pass you can take a side dirt road that goes another mile or two up to the top at about 7500 feet. It's a soft rounded top covered in pine forest. On the East side there's a sudden and impressive drop off to about 4000 feet. This is the Verde Valley. Up on this somewhat flat wooded area are a number of church camps, cabins, and other youth camps.

Back to the road that winds over the Mountain, it takes a slightly less sudden, but very windy path down the East side. About a third of the way down is the tiny mining town of

Jerome. There are few other towns that so deserve the description "perched on the side of a mountain".

From there the road gets to a gentler drop down into the Verde Valley and the towns of Clarkdale, Cottonwood, and beyond that to Sedona.

Max grew up on the East side, down in Clarkdale and up in Jerome.

John

John was born in Prescott in 1949 and lived here until 4th grade. Then his father got a job in Phoenix and he lived there the rest of his childhood. He describes himself as a wild kid who got in fights and could easily have ended up in a lot of trouble.

Gordon

Gordon was born in 1950 and his family moved to Prescott when he was 11 months old. At that time Prescott had less than 7,000 people. Now it and some surrounding towns have arisen or grown so Prescott and its neighboring towns are thought of as the Prescott area. But then Prescott pretty much stood alone, and was a rural town and a center for surrounding cattle ranches.

Brad

Brad is the youngster of the group, born in 1952. He starts his story with an idyllic childhood in Arizona. Mostly in Phoenix, with later summers in the Prescott area. One of eight children, five boys and three girls. Growing up was in some ways an accurate reflection of a Western state growing with the times. His father worked for Air Research, part of the modern industry that was growing at the time. While his father was involved in the new world of technology, Brad grew up with a foot in an earlier time, spending as much time as possible on horseback.

His older sister, Mary, spent several summers at a camp at Mountain Meadows Ranch, one of those camps on Mingus Mountain. It is a beautiful mountain-top location covered in pine and, in the winter, snow.

The family would drive up together. The road was dirt and rough and dropped off sharply on one side. His mother would fret to his father that it was dangerous. His father, to pass the time on the trip, would tell Brad why it was named Mingus Mountain, and made up a story about a creature called the Mingus. It was big and hairy and would capture a little boy and tickle him terribly if he didn't keep his campsite clean. The story went that there weren't many Mingus creatures because the boys of the Mingus would run around the mountain clockwise and the girls would run the other way, so they rarely met. This is as close to information about the birds and bees as his father ever spoke.

Back in Phoenix life was regulated. Promptly at 6 o'clock dinner started and children were expected to have something to say about there day. One evening his father told of visiting a school during the day. He was involved in a United Way fund-raising campaign and had gone to Valley of the Sun School. It is a school and rehabilitation center still in service today. His father was quite moved by the hardship of these kids with serious problems. This made an impression on Brad which he still remembers. Though he also remember that he was eager to be done with dinner and get back to his horse which was tied up out front.

What his father said that day was one of two memories from Brad's childhood that made strong impressions that later related to his work. The other memory is of a Superman show. It was in black and white. Superman and a young girl in braces and a wheelchair were pitted against the bad guys. The bad guys abducted the young girl and took her braces off, which made her cry terribly. Later, of course, Superman saved her and the bad guys got what they deserved. The girl was still in her braces and wheelchair but she was all right. So although Superman couldn't fix her legs, he had helped her and it was a good ending.

Before long there were signs that Brad, who was happy-go-lucky on the one hand, was not going to be one to take things as they were. He was a true 60's kid. As early as junior high school he was agitating for integration. As he says, "agitating like a jerk kid as if I knew anything about anything." It was the start of a pattern of taking action to try to make a difference.

HIGH SCHOOL

For Kathy and Brad and John high school meant Catholic high
school in Phoenix. Two of the Catholic high schools there,
Brophy for the boys, and Xavier for the girls, were run by the
Jesuit order of priests, and nuns from the order of The Blessed
Virgin Mary, and had a role in the background of all three.
They were in slightly different years at the school but were at
the least aware of one another.

Kathy

The influence of school on her awareness of those in need continued and became stronger in high school. At Xavier she received a deeper than normal education in religion, and a great deal of reinforcement of the idea of social responsibility. The Jesuits, rather than just teaching the usual mechanics of catechism, dug into the philosophy of it and reasons behind the Catholic view so their students had more intellectual tools to support their faith. They apparently did a good enough job that she can remember sitting in church and wondering why there was so much more talk than action.

Her parents sent her to Xavier because it was a good Catholic school, and simply out of wanting to send her to the best school they could.

It was generally assumed at Xavier that most of the students would be going on to college, though there were those who chose not to and took slightly different curriculum not aimed at college. In her Freshman year Kathy didn't do so well; her challenge with concentration making it difficult. As a result a counselor advised she not plan on college. Never tell Kathy she can't do something. She got mad, and set her sites on college. Her course of interests would have led her to college anyway, but this incident was typical of her reaction to being thwarted, and brought her to a conscious decision about college.

It was not that she felt smart and just naturally college material. None of her older siblings had gone to college yet

22

and her parents were ambivalent about it. Setting her sites on college was partly the influence of standards and expectations of Xavier, and partly Kathy's personality coming through. Here tendency, without even thinking about it, was to simply be aware that there were things that needed doing and that she had her part to play, and that she expected to do that part. Planning on college was just an obvious step in that process.

John

John's high school experience had two particularly formative aspects. That Brophy school diverted him from being a kid in a lot of fights and trouble, and possibly headed for jail otherwise. The other was his work for a family friend in Nogales at a veterinarian clinic two Summers.

John is the most religious of the group, his Catholicism staying strong throughout his life. Getting well set on that path was in large part due to attending Brophy.

Nogales is a city about three hours South East of Phoenix. It is right on the border and overlaps, part in Arizona and part in Sonora, Mexico. Now it's about 20,000 people. Then it was a much smaller, rustic border town.

For a couple of the Summers during high school he went to Nogales. A high school friend of his father's had a veterinarian clinic there. Starting here he developed an interest in science, but it also brought out his tendency to just be interested in all sorts of things. He said that tendency stuck with him into adult life to the point it would sometimes drive his wife crazy. That he had so many diverse interests he would get absorbed in. From car engines, to carving, to coin collecting, to rock lapidary.

He enjoyed working with the animals, but also the science of it. They would dissect dogs that had died just so he could learn the anatomy of them.

He also got his first taste of psychology. The veterinarians wife had some books on it that he read and got him interested in it.

He also saw what college held as far as possibilities for pursuing science. A couple of the guys who helped there were Hispanic friends he would hang out with and play sports and such. They were both in college in the sciences. One went on to a Phd in agriculture and the other became a veterinarian. They both impressed him as very bright and their studies in science interested him.

During his sophomore year he considered becoming a priest. As he put it, though, he, "liked girls too much." He then went through a period of the church not having much influence on his life, from this point up until marriage. Then the influence of the church in his background came back to be an important part of his life.

Max, Gordon, Don

Max was going to Mingus Union High School, when it was still in Jerome. It has since moved to Cottonwood down in the Verde Valley.

Gordon was going to Prescott High School. His dad owned the well known Glau Gas Heating and Cooling company. In the Summers he worked there.

Don was going to the tiny high school in Illinois. There were 30 people in his class, including his future wife, Judy.

Brad

Brad was several years behind Kathy but can remember her, and remember wanting to ask her out. He did once and he remembers that she laughed, perhaps not sure how to respond to him or whether he was serious. He just took it that she was an upper-classman, and gorgeous, and that going out with her was not in the cards. Years later, in Prescott, at Brads 40th birthday party Kathleen attended in a prom dress since back in school he had wanted to take her to the prom.

He also knew a couple of students from Prescott who were bordered there at Brophy, Tom and Dan Rusing. That connection would prove important later.

During his high school years Brad continued a pattern of not being one to take things as they came, or take it easy. He was student body leader and active in draft resistance. He was definitely attuned to the idea of wanting to make a difference.

During this same period the camp his sister had gone to was to play an important role. Brad started working at the camp in the summers, riding horses, fixing fences, and helping with the camp kids.

A few years later it would play another important role. At the end of his high school senior year, as student body leader, and just as he was about to give a speech at one of the end-of-the-year events, the president of the school announced that a camp up near Prescott was going to become the Easter Seals camp for physically handicapped children, and that they needed volunteers. To Brad it was like lighting striking. Those threads of what his father had said, and of those feelings for the girl in the wheelchair, and this opening to help, came together in an instant of clarity in which he felt that that is what he should be doing; helping children with disabilities.

This making a decision in a moment and jumping in is typical of Brad. He seems to be more of a doer than a thinker. There is actually more thought going on than he lets appear on the surface, but to make a quick decision and go for it is obviously an innate trait from early on.

So when he heard about the need for volunteers at the Easter Seals camp, and the notion struck him that that is what he should be doing, that was it. He was on his way.

It turned out that the camp was that same camp he'd been working at, and which was now going to be become a more specialized camp for these children. As soon as he could, he showed up at the camp on the door of Mr. Henry Dahlberg who owned it. Mr. Dahlberg was just a young man of 25 himself at the time, but Brad was well his junior. Brad said to him, "You have these handicapped kids coming, you're the director, I have the horse and the guitar..." and so the first phase of his work with disadvantaged people began.

The work with the children at the camp was typical camp events. To start with he took some along with him while he did cowboy work, riding and tending fences and such. It evolved into more organized activity, set schedules for groups to do arts and crafts, swim, ride and work with the horses, and other activities.

Brad would ask the kids at the camp what they did the rest of the year back home. Generally the answer was that they hung around home and did nothing, or they were in a state institution.

Over the next several summers, continuing on into college, this work grew, and the length of the camps grew, from two weeks to twelve weeks. Brad also met his future wife there.

COLLEGE

Don

In 1963 Don graduated high school, and that Fall started college at Southern Illinois University. He was one of four or five out of his high school class of 30 that went on to college. Most of the families had farms. His family lived in the town. Since he wasn't going from high school to the farm he needed another plan.

Part of the consideration was that college was a way to get a deferment from getting drafted and almost certainly going to Vietnam. That was a very real consideration. As it turned out, one of their high school class did die as a result of the war. Until going to college he was pretty much ready to go to the war if drafted. But since he wasn't going to a farm, and college seemed the next thing to do, and it also was a deferment, the package of the next logical step and a deferment seemed like the thing to do.

As he said, when considering where in his mind the story starts, "Well for me the story starts when I was dislodged from the Mid-West by the war in Vietnam". This was the first step in that process.

While he was at the university he wasn't sure what career he wanted to go for, just that it would be some sort of helping profession. What that would be he didn't know, he says partly from growing up in an isolated town and not knowing of many career paths to consider.

He had a small scholarship with few strings attached. As a student he was doing okay. As he approached the end of his time at college his small, hometown draft board was actively nipping at his heals. They expected him to go. These were people who knew his family. They were getting impatient.

As he was at college his horizons began to open up a little bit, met other people, saw people protesting, saw booths in the student union about how to avoid the draft, and he was very conflicted about it. To him that was to be expected, being conflicted about it. But he did start to think that maybe he didn't want to go there, that maybe he should try to avoid combat.

He doesn't think that was unusual. As he sees it, draft dodgers then, and even now, were viewed negatively, but actually a lot of people who were claiming at the time to be patriotic were like him, conflicted. While truly feeling patriotic about their country, they weren't so sure that going to war in Vietnam was really the best they could do for their country. Many of these people were doing anything they could to avoid the draft, having kids, going to school, getting a particular kind of job, joining the National Guard.

He and his future wife, Judy, were in love and talking about when to get married. If he did go to Vietnam should they get married before or after that? During this time, with his interest in some helping profession, he gravitated toward social work and wanting to do advanced studies in it. He thinks that interest may have been kindled by some professors who modeled that profession for him, a profession he hadn't known existed. With interest kindled he joined a social-work club on the campus and met people pursuing the field.

During this time President Kennedy had made community based mental health care a priority for his administration. The Community Mental Health Centers Act brought a huge infusion of federal support to states to assist in establishing community mental health centers nationwide. This brought funding, jobs and accelerated training programs to provide qualified professional staff. Don ended up with a full ride graduate scholarship in Social Work at the University of Tennessee in Nashville.

So Don went off to the University of Tennessee in Nashville for graduate work. The next step in his being "dislodged" from the Mid-West.

He and Judy were married between the first and second year of studies there.

Meanwhile his hometown draft board was still bearing down, determined to draft him. They were getting more impatient with him because he was doing things that rarely happened, like filing appeals, and running out appeals. He got pretty adept at it. He would wait until some hearing was just about due and then he would introduce some new item into his file, which would require that they review it, setting the schedule back. He was trying to string it out so he could get through graduate school.

While wanting to finish school, he also figured he would end up serving in some capacity, and he was ready and willing to serve, he just didn't want to serve as a "grunt". So while the draft board was still trying to draft him, he was applying to various branches of the service for other kinds of service. He applied to be a pilot or navigator. He says he "stupidly" thought that would be better. In hind site he says he probably would be dead if he had become a pilot.

That plan didn't work. He washed out of applying to be a pilot because his eyes weren't good enough. He washed out of trying to be a navigator "because of my aversion to mathematics".

Part of his reason for applying for these other service options was to demonstrate to his draft board that he really did intend to serve, just not until school was done, and not as a "grunt".

Then he noticed an important little ad. It was in the student lounge. It said that the Public Health Service, Commissioned Corp was looking for social workers. It also said it would satisfy the military service obligation.

This corp is one of the uniform service branches of the U.S. Just as the Army and Navy are, the Coast Guard is, and so is this corp. Do you remember in the 1980s the Surgeon General was C. Everett Koop, who often appeared in uniform? It's that corp. The corp is uniformed branch of the US Public Health Service. The Commissioned Corps is under the direct authority of the Surgeon General and is assigned in areas of special healthcare needs: Indian Health, Centers for Disease Control, Bureau of Prisons and other federal agencies. In fact, the

Commissioned Corps was also assigned to Vietnam during the early stages of the war when the US was trying to win the hearts and minds of the Vietnamese people by providing health care to villages throughout the country.

Don applied, was accepted, and became a commissioned officer in the corp. He says it was a blessing for Judy and he because he had a way to continue his career, he and Judy could be together, and he was in the military. Moving to his first commission for the corp completed his being "dislodged" from the Mid-West. We'll come to that.

Later in life, with a different perspective, Don would say, "I have grown in my appreciation and respect for those who did serve in Vietnam. With time and perspective I have become increasingly comfortable with my response to the Vietnam War and the draft. Like most men of my age, I knew the war was awful and I tried to avoid the worst of it, but I never tried to avoid military service. In fact, I took three separate physicals trying to get into Officers Candidate School. In the end, I served and served honorably and am glad I did."

Kathy

Kathy started Arizona State University in Phoenix in 1967. For a while she was split between her interest in the helping professions and art. She considered becoming an architect but decided sociology was her better choice.

She and Mike Murphy had been dating for a long time and then engaged. During her last year in college he was at law school. She had been very opposed to the war and remembers talking about going into the Peace Corp as a couple after they were married. Mike never approved of the war and didn't understand it. While in law school Mike's draft number came up and he expected to end up going. A potential heart problem, though, was found during his physical and he ended up not being drafted.

In her last year she started work at a juvenile detention center. Work which continued after her graduation. She was the first employee with a degree. The focus had been basic maintenance of order and a system of punishment for control. They were just at the point of wanting to change that to a more behavioral modification system, which is part of the reason they hired her. That gave her a goal, to try to bring them into a better way of doing things. She says if the job had simply been to be part of the old structure she wouldn't have taken the job.

It was here she first became very aware that what these kids needed more than help while in the detention center, was help before hand so they didn't end up their in the first place.

She continued working at the detention center until they moved to Prescott.

Max

In 1967 Max graduated from Mingus Union high school in Jerome. That Fall he started college at Northern Arizona University in Flagstaff. Flagstaff is a city about an hour North of the Verde valley, and several thousand feet higher. It gets serious snow all Winter in town, and up on the nearby mountainside of the San Francisco Peaks is a good ski area. At that time there were around 30,000 people there, about half what it is now.

He worked his way through college, spending most weekends and Summer breaks at Tuzigoot National Monument. It's in the Verde Valley and is centered on the remnants of walls from Native American pueblos built 1000 years ago. It's a hot, dry place to spend a Summer day outside. Sometimes 120 degrees. He and the rest of the crew did hard manual maintenance labor. Sometimes hauling concrete used to stabilize the structure.

There were a couple of youths working with him there from the Neighborhood Youth Corp. He got to supervise them. This is part of where he got his interest in working with kids.

The Youth Corp was a big thing in the 60s. His experience of the 60s was of a lot of interest in people wanting to do something positive. Something for change. That influenced him.

In 1971 he graduated from NAU with a bachelors degree in sociology. During the Summer he and Lindsay were married.

Lindsay would later also play a role in social services in Prescott, with the West Yavapai Guidance clinic and being involved with other groups.

It was after he had his bachelor's degree that he realized he needed a masters degree to get a good job.

In 1972 he started on his masters degree in sociology at ASU in Phoenix. During the first year of masters program he was assigned to work at a nursing home in Tucson. He would work there two days a week, and got to know some of the people and got attached to them.

He found it depressing that people he got to know there died. That made him all the more interested in working with youth. During the 2nd year of the program he was placed with Child Protective Services, then called the Welfare Department.

In 1973 he graduated with his masters degree.

John

John graduated from high school in 1968 and started college at the University of Arizona in Tucson. His studies and interests in college were a process of sorting out his interest in science —mostly laboratory science—and working with people.

He was pursuing a dual degree, combined biology and chemistry, and psychology. Where those studies best came together was in physiological psychology. Putting electrical probes into rat's brains and running tests and that sort of thing. It was also in this field that he had one of his most inspiring teachers.

This range of study had him involved in a couple of different departments at the school and he saw a difference in approach. In the agricultural department he took all the genetics courses he could. Of course genetic studies at that time were about results of breeding and such and not about the direct genetic manipulations that are done today, but it did hold a fascination for him just learning the science of various animals.

At the same time he was taking courses in the psychology department. He noticed an interesting contrast between them. The psychology department treated their students the worst, seeming to not offer much help for them to succeed. On the other hand the agricultural department was the best on campus in his estimation, for having a supportive atmosphere and helping students along.

During this time he went to mass only occasionally. He did sometimes work for the church though.

While he was working across these various fields, "I was watching students who were great at the psychology and thinking I couldn't do that. But the physiological psychology, putting probes into rat brains and such, never bothered me. Originally I was not thinking of working with people, for a variety of reasons, including being fascinated by some of the science I had studied. I think I felt like I wouldn't be very good at working with people and would be better at science. I like people and always had a lot of friends and such but felt more competent at science. Looking back on that it was kind of silly because I don't think I was as competent in that, but I really liked it. It was fun, interesting, stimulating."

Toward the end of the time at UofA he and Joan were married. Shortly after that he graduated with the psychology degree.

During this time his connection with the church would occasionally come back to him. Every time he found himself in need he would turn to the church and somehow it would work out. He recalls a little later on, when we had a young child on the way and no job, he was in a church in Tucson praying when a guy walked in and gave him a job as a janitor there. "I always liked the church environment. Never had a drive to make a ton of money. It just didn't appeal to me. So the church was always in the back of my mind."

Having completed that degree, a good friend, Oscar, told him about the advanced psychology program at ASU that he had just completed. John applied and started on a masters in counseling.

The draft was an issue for him, but less pressing. When the lottery came out he got number 273. He figured that meant they'd be down to taking little old ladies by the time they got to him. He was in that split state of mind that seemed to be common. He would have gone if he was drafted. It wouldn't have conflicted with his faith because the church allowed for what was considered necessary combat.

At the same time he would not have wanted to go. Joan had participated in anti-war marches in San Francisco. Some of their friends were hippies. Before long there was also another factor, they had had their son Shane.

Joan was a very strong part of what was frequent in mainstream religions at the time, the combination of being anti-war, strong social activism, and very active in the church. She was lead singer at their college mass. She received $25 a month from her parents and she would send part of that off to some mission. This added to John's reconnection to the church. As he put it, "At one point when newly married Joan was going to church and said, 'Let's go', and I said I wasn't. She insisted that we both go, and I went." From that point on he has been constantly involved in the church.

As he was studying for the counseling degree he would be the first to volunteer for the most challenging counseling cases the students were given. One case was a man who had been convicted of killing a boy. Another was the first sex abuse case he or any of the students had encountered. He would jump at these because, "It was exciting to get in there and see what you can do."

When not studying he worked at landscaping to bring in an income. Later in his studies he worked at the Franciscan

Renewal Center, called Casa. He graduated with the counseling degree, and continued working at Casa.

Gordon

Gordon started at Northern Arizona University in Flagstaff in 1968. He was going for a Police Science degree. He got into it thinking of some kind of federal law enforcement. He was not interested in local law enforcement. He had in mind working for the FBI or Secret Service, or the CIA, or, "something kind of grandiose".

He remembers the Vietnam war becoming a bigger issue around his Junior year. They were using the lottery system at that time and he got number 187. There was that federal draft number, which he knew, but there was also a local draft board number. You never got to know that one. When that number came up they let you know and you had to go into the service quick.

He remembers around Christmas time that year he heard Walter Cronkite on the news. He was saying that if you notified the draft board that you were forgoing your college deferment, that they had one year for your number to come up. If it didn't come up during that year then you would not be drafted in the future. He still isn't sure if that was true, but it's what he did.

As it turns out his number never came up. If it had come up he's not sure he would have gone. "I was very rebellious in those days. There were a lot of demonstrations and civil unrest. There were a lot of liberal professors. Even though I was in a very conservative major, Police Science, I was minoring in political science and sociology and psychology.

So I got a pretty good array of humanity, and what was going on."

"I've always had somewhat of a rebellious streak. Not just accepting the status quo. Challenge that, and push the envelope a little bit, and ask the question 'Why?' 'Why can you? Why can't you? Why can't I do this?'"

After his Junior year Gordon and Pattie Kelly married. Pattie is a native of Prescott and they had been high school sweethearts. Pattie was a year ahead of Gordon and graduated college in 1971.

In his senior year he started taking classes in corrections and social service areas. He also found some classes on probation. His memory is that the sociology/psychology/political science part of the curriculum was automatic with a major in police science. In any case it gave him some exposure to social service. "There was a professor named Brad Lynn who had a small case load of kids on probation and I interned with him and supervised some of those kids. That's where I really started generating a lot of interest in doing that. I was in a minority in police science. A lot of these were gun-toting guys who wanted to get out there and be cops. There were a few of us that were in it for something different."

With that, his focus broadened. He still intended to try for federal jobs, but now he was also open to juvenile probation jobs anywhere in Arizona. He had never really wanted to be a police officer, but rather that allure of leaving the small town, moving to a big city, and doing something dangerous and important like being an FBI agent. At the same time he had an interest in service. These conflicting pieces of his interest were working themselves out. Of his interest in service he says it, "was probably just upbringing. Your environment around you affects what direction you're going to go, and I wanted to make a difference. I don't know where I got that, other than my upbringing. I wanted to help kids as it turned out. I had the view at that point that there were all kinds of injustices and they were locking them all up and I'm going to save the world. But I don't think that was that uncommon to have that viewpoint in that era. I wanted to get out there and save the world. That's why I did it. I think the whole environment, of family, and living here, as well as the era, led towards that."

Of the fading allure of the big city and an FBI job he says, "At some point it dawned on me I wanted to help kids rather than get into the big bureaucracy of government. Growing up in a small town there were dreams of going to the big city and doing something exciting and dangerous. Then reality starts to set in, and what do you really want to do? I never thought I'd stay in Prescott. Growing up here, everybody wants to leave. But I love it here."

He continued to work at his dad's Glau Gas Heating and Cooling during the Summers.

Brad

As high school came to an end, in 1971, and decisions about college and what was next needed to be made, good timing was happening elsewhere. Just at this time rehabilitation was becoming a strong theme in social services. In 1973 the rehabilitation movement was getting started and the Rehabilitation Act of 1973 became law. As a consequence the University of Arizona in Tucson started a department for special education and rehabilitation. Brad and some friends who were interested in social service decided they would all go down there and get degrees.

During college he continued to work for Easters Seals and learned quite a bit from it. From running the camp he learned about running an organization. He also learned about fund-raising and the importance of community connections and how to develop them. Plus he learned to not lose focus on what the goal was; to have a good relationship with the kids and stay attuned to whether it was all working well for them.

The director of Easter Seals emphasized to him that paying attention to the business end of a charity was important. "You can't help kids if there are no funds in the bank" he would say.

While a graduate student in Tucson the head of the department invited him to a seminar with the executive director of CARF, the Commission on Accreditation of Rehabilitation Facilities. There he learned the value of a new concept, national accreditation. At that time rehab centers generally weren't accredited. They had to meet certain standards if they wanted to get state money to help their income. Meeting state standards was part of the process, but rehab centers were not typically accredited. This was something new and something Brad thought would be valuable for a rehab center to achieve.

Just before he was due to graduate with his degree in social services he came across a job he couldn't refuse. Stuck on the bulletin board at school was a small note about a job as director of a rehab center in Prescott. He snatched the note off the board and applied and got the job.

He and his young wife and child went to Prescott, abandoning the degree he was close to getting.

STARTING CAREERS

Don

Don's first commission as an officer of the Public Health Service was in Pine Ridge, South Dakota. For someone who hadn't been West of the Mississippi, this completed his being "dislodged" from the Mid-West in a big way.

As part of that corp he could have ended up any number of places, from an urban health clinic to Alaska. Many of the openings at that time, though, were for Native American health clinics. The hospital in Pine Ridge had an opening and called and offered it to him, and he took it. He was very excited because wherever this place was, it wasn't Vietnam.

Immediately after the phone call he went to a bookstore and bought an atlas so he could look up where Pine Ridge, South Dakota was. The next thing he did was to call Judy and tell her. Then he called his mom. He told her they were going to

South Dakota and he didn't need to worry about Vietnam anymore. She asked him if he was sure that was the right thing to do.

They were very excited about the opening because there were a lot of job openings around the Mid-West and he had been recruited by some of them that would have fit right in with staying in the region if that's what they had wanted to do. Now they were going to go do something completely different.

The time came and they packed up and made the trip West. Since they hadn't been West there was a lot of seeing regions new to them for the first time. Don remembers he and Judy going through Scotts Bluff, Nebraska and seeing what appeared to be Native Americans for the first time.

They arrived in Pine Ridge and quickly found themselves in a wonderful situation. There was a sixty bed hospital that served the reservation, and a housing compound right next door for the staff. There were about thirty couples, "just like us. Living in a housing compound adjacent to the hospital. We had a wonderful little house with a yard and all that. Very bright people from all over the country. Most of them side-stepping the draft and Vietnam. Mostly young doctors, dentists, pharmacists, and other social workers. It was just wonderful from all sorts of perspectives. For the first time we really got to know people of other backgrounds and religions. Jewish people, Italians, people from the East Coast who spoke a different dialect. I was working side by side with doctors, and they were my friends and we played together, we socialized together, we traveled together. In the Summers, on Wednesday nights, we would have a pot luck and everyone would come out into the compound, bring a dish, drink beer, and play volleyball. It was very special."

It was great from that perspective. It was also challenging in the work. "We were plunked right in the middle of one of the most dynamic reservations in the country. Still is in many ways. It's Wounded Knee. It's one of the most impoverished reservations, still to this day. It wasn't easy in that sense, but what an experience. I was assigned to the hospital as a hospital social worker, had a little department. The chief social worker, right out of grad school." The hospital dealt with a lot of trauma cases. "Almost all trauma in that hospital. Or very serious infectious diseases, especially TB." The hospital also delivered a lot of babies. "There were also a lot of suicide attempts, which got me interested in dealing with that."

They were also quite connected to the community and exploring the area. "We did a lot of hunting and fishing and spending time with Native Americans."

Don worked in the hospital for a year. Then an opportunity came. Right across the parking lot was the first community mental health center to be set up on a reservation in the country and Don's assignment moved over there. "It was heavily funded by the federal government as a pilot program. We had three social workers, a psychiatrist, a psychiatric nurse, a doctorate level anthropologist, and a sociologist. We then developed a program for para-professionals mental health workers that we trained to work with us. Native Americans who we hired for the positions. We did a lot of research. Kind of felt our way through it because we were a pilot program. We did a lot of work in the community, a lot of teaching. I taught a high school class at the school which was all Ogalala Sioux. We were real interested in customs, and traditional medicine, so we had exposure to that. We would sponsor ceremonies. We had a Yuwipi ceremony intended to end the war in Vietnam, conducted by Frank Fools Crow, a prominent holy man among the Ogalala."

In his second year there Don became director of the facility. He stayed on for a total of four years.

During the time they explored the West. Their work schedule gave them stretches of time off and they would jump in the car and drive to Montana and Colorado and Arizona and the West Coast.

"There were three medicine men I became acquainted with there." They were Frank Fools Crows, Pete Catches, and Ben Black Elk. Don also had a beer once there with Russell Means, the radical leader of the American Indian Movement.

A little side-note here. You may remember in 1973 a group of Native Americans took over a small town on a reservation and had a stand-off with federal authorities for several months? That was this reservation. The incident happened not long after Don and his wife had moved on to their next job. The towns of Pine Ridge and Wounded Knee are on the reservation. Wounded Knee was the site of a famous massacre of Native Americans in 1890. One of those who was there then was revered medicine man, Black Elk. Black Elk's son was Ben Black Elk. Pete Catches was a medicine man when Don was there. His grandfather had survived the original Wounded Knee massacre because he was a nine year old boy who was told to run down a dry creek bed to get away. Frank Fools Crows was another medicine man and nephew of Black Elk. He helped negotiate the end of the 1973 stand-off. Russell Means was one of the leaders of the incident. He was indicted, but not convicted based on "prosecutorial misconduct".

"Ben Black Elk later kind of sold his soul. If you went to Mount Rushmore for a price you could get your picture taken with him."

"When we arrived in Pine Ridge there was a very amiable relationship between the non-Indian professionals and the local people. It was a very comfortable atmosphere. You could go anywhere on the reservation. You were always safe, there was no fear whatsoever. But Wounded Knee changed all that. It divided that reservation and the results has been a lot of animosity against whites."

"I remember having a beer with Russel Means, who was a pain in the ass to all of us because he was trying to make trouble. And he succeeded. That's when that split began to happen."

"My military obligation was now fulfilled. I looked at a job in Florida, and was ultimately recruited in Arizona by a fellow who had served before me in SD and who is still a dear friend. So I came out to AZ and worked for the White Mountain Apache Tribe, because I had that tribal experience now, and kind of knew the territory of working with Native Americans. So that brought us to Arizona and we've been here ever since."

During this time they lived in Pine Top. Working at White Mountain was a lot different. "That was hard. That was brutal. A very different experience. The cultures I found to be very different. The Apache just seem to have a level of latent animosity and anger that just always seemed to be there. With the Sioux it felt like you were truly kind of accepted and there wasn't an issue, but it always was at White Mountain."

He was there about three years. "I was ultimately fired by a new tribal chairman, Ronnie Lupe, who has gone on to be president of that tribe for many many years, on and off. That opened the door here, and I came to Prescott in 1976."

"We expected, again, that we would stay a few years and move on. My mom and dad were hoping we would move back to the Mid-West because they were missing us, and we had kids."

"I still believe it starts back there at that critical turning point that sent us West. It could have sent us North West or to Alaska, but it happened to send us to South Dakota."

Lindsay Bell, Max Bell's wife, was board president at WYGC at that time and it was her board that hired Don.

Gordon

Pattie and Gordon honeymooned in Europe for 3 months. After he graduated from college the following year, they returned to Europe for another 3 months with his parents. As a way to make money upon their return, Gordon and his wife were selling jewelry. Gordon's cousin, Rick Collins, hired them on commission and had found someone in California to put up some financing. They would buy good quality Indian Jewelry from Gilbert Ortega in Gallup, New Mexico. They would travel around the state selling this jewelry.

He was also applying for the federal law enforcement jobs as he had planned, but also for juvenile probation openings around the state. It was a good thing he had become interested in juvenile probation in school because it turned out that the FBI, at that time, was more interested in hiring accountants and lawyers and going after white-collar crime. They weren't doing much hiring of undergraduates.

He did get an interview scheduled with the Secret Service. While he was waiting for that he ran into a guy he knew in town by the name of Merle Klefkorn. Merle had a gas station in town. Merle told him he had just left a juvenile probation officer position. If Gordon was interested he should go on down there. So he beat it down there and applied.

He ended up with an interview for that job before his scheduled interview with the Secret Service came up. He interviewed with Everett Boyer who was the chief probation officer. Paul Rosenblatt was the presiding judge at the time, now a U.S. District Court Judge. He did a second interview with Gordon.

They hired him. It was a bit of a stretch for them to hire someone so young and just out of college. The position in the past had typically been filled by someone retired from law enforcement. At the time juvenile probation was heavily geared toward enforcement as contrasted with rehabilitation.

Juvenile probation was being done by Everett and one other officer, Dean Wolfe, and Merle who had just left. The Yavapai probation department and the Coconino department worked pretty closely together, and that department had hired a young man recently and he had worked out well. Everett had it down to Gordon or a guy in Phoenix, and decided to go with Gordon. June sixteenth 1973 he started.

When he started, it was a pretty basic operation. "Early on, all the juvenile probation cases were kept in a ledger book. A kid would come in to do his check-in and a checkmark would be put in the book. There were no programs really, just supervision and the guidance the probation officers could pass on. If there was need for any in-depth counseling, that was done by the Guidance Clinic."

"In fact it was Everett and Judge Ogg who were instrumental in getting the Guidance Clinic going. They were advocates for that along with Jean Phillips, a local community activist. Otherwise, to convince kids to change lifestyle we kind of flew by the seat of our pants."

"We reached into the community for resources. We had some families who would occasionally take a kid in, almost like free foster care. It was a great learning experience because Everett and Dean, if they taught me one lesson it was this; to treat people with respect, regardless of who they are, what they've done. Coming from a strong law enforcement mentality it was kind of refreshing; that these are human beings. I don't care if they're the biggest drug addict in the world, or very aggressive, you treat them with dignity and respect, as a human being. You hold them accountable, certainly. It doesn't mean you're going to soften your behavior, but you treat them decently. That stayed with me throughout my career and I tried to instill that in my people."

"We had an office in the county courthouse on the top floor, where there are courtrooms now. There were three offices, and the jail was on that floor too. The one cell for male juveniles was right next to the one cell for adult females. You can imagine the cat calls and things that would go on. Then right over the judges quarters was the female juvenile cell which was more like an apartment, with bars on the outside windows. The jail was also responsible for detention. I was responsible for taking the male juveniles to the showers each day. But there was no program, no exercise. We'd take them into our office to talk to them some but other than that they were in their cells. Plans were underway to build a new facility where it is now on Division Street."

"Early on, in October, only a few months after I got there, we had a suicide. It almost stopped my career because I was pretty well devastated about it. "

"But I got through it, and then pretty shortly, in 1972, we moved into our new facility, and things moved on."

Max

When Max was completing his masters in sociology part of his training was work at what was then called the Welfare Department in Phoenix. Traditionally it had been part of the Welfare Department's job to work with mothers and young children, to try to get the mothers into the workforce. In the course of that they sometimes had to deal with cases of neglect or abuse. That's what Max was helping with. It was about this time the state started to split off the Child Protective Services into their own department.

Before it was split off the CPS function was part of a slate of services welfare applicants received. The focus was mainly on single mothers, and the idea was to provide them with child care, job training, and other services that would lead to them getting of off welfare. Max remembers that the Nixon administration had pretty progressive, expansive policies on this.

He applied to, and was hired by, the Yavapai County Welfare Department, starting in June, 1973. "When I was first hired the job paid $8000 a year." After he was done with school and the jobs he had through that, they were living off Lindsay's minimum wage job. "When I got the first pay check from the new job I cashed it just for the fun of taking it home and throwing it up in the air."

He and another new hire replaced what had been the one child protective worker in the county. Max's new territory was half of Prescott area and all of the Verde Valley.

When he started they might get four or five allegations or referrals of abuse or neglect a month, between the two of them. Their home numbers were given to police and hospitals, and they would trade off 24-hour shifts of being on-call. Since there were no cell phones that meant staying near the phone.

The Welfare Department also had one adoption worker, one foster-home licensing worker, one day-care worker, and a supervisor. They also provided adult protective services, for instance for battered wives, and protective service for the developmentally disabled.

The difference in size and case load back then he puts down partly to population growth, but also that people just weren't as aware of child abuse then.

One thing that hasn't changed is controversy, and the need to be thick skinned and just do the job as seems best. CPS always has to walk the line of when to protect kids versus when to try to help the kids be with their family, which is what they almost always want to do. When to help the family reform and end whatever abuse or neglect is going on and become a more functional family. They are constantly under pressure from both sides, that they should remove kids quicker to protect them, and that they remove them too quickly and break up families. They have to take in what impressions and information they can in a short amount of time with the children and the families, and make their best judgment. "You do have to look at the child, at what risk of what damage, what is the risk to the child. To stay child focused and family focused. Where can that child best live and have a protected, positive kind of a childhood? Sometimes that's not going to be with the parent, but sometimes it can be with the parent even though they've had pretty significant issues."

Max remembers cases even back then where he would hear from people in the community on both sides about a given child, that they should be removed, and that it would be terrible to break up the family. "You just have to ignore the pressure and focus on the child and the family and what's best for the kid. If the parents are responsive to treatment they should be given a chance. If not, sever the relationship and place the kids in permanent homes elsewhere. If the abuse or neglect was too bad the parents may not deserve a second chance. But kids want to be with their parents."

For the first six years Max did either CPS work or adoptions, placing children in adoptive homes, doing the placement studies, and such. After six years he became supervisor, and supervised all of Yavapai County.

Kathleen

In 1974 Kathleen went to her first meeting of the local Big Brothers organization. She had already been interested in Big Brothers/Big Sisters from her time working at the detention center in Phoenix before moving to Prescott. "The reason I wanted to get into working with BBBS was from my time working at the detention center. These kids had a lot of emotional needs, and it didn't seem like a good approach to me to wait until they were in trouble to get them services. I remember thinking this doesn't make a lot of sense. Here we are spending millions of dollars on these kids and half of what they need is friendship. They need someone to talk to, someone to listen to them and almost all of the kids there were from single parent homes. I remember thinking about that, and then I heard about BBBS, and I heard that once in a while one of these kids would get a Big. So I knew about the organization. It made a lot of sense to me."

Many people who have heard of the organization have a vague sense of what it does, or even confuse it with other organizations. BBBS is a mentoring service, matching adults with children who need a little more adult influence in their lives. Children are referred to BBBS by teachers, or because they have a parent in prison, or if they start to get into trouble and the juvenile legal systems sees that part of their problem is a need for more adult influence. They are mostly children with one parent available, sometimes both grandparents or other relatives are there, but are glad to have a mentor for their child if they feel they're not up to providing what's needed. Some are children with problems and many are not.

The children ("Littles") and their parent are interviewed to see what the need is and what the parent approves of (for instance do they care what religion the "Big" is?). Volunteer adults ("Bigs") are carefully screened and checked and matched with a Little so that the two are likely to be a good match. The Big simply spends time with the Little, maybe just a couple of hours a month. Maybe just throwing a ball. Maybe talking about important things or maybe not, or just listening. Match Adviser stay in touch with both the Big and the Little and monitor progress, and support the Big in how to be successful at it. The match may go on for a year, or in many case go on until the Little is an adult, and in some cases the two stay involved almost like a grandparent and grandchild, long into the Little's life. This simple involvement of an extra adult makes a huge, and documented, difference in the number of these children who turn out well, as shall be seen.

"Someone got my husband involved as a Big when we were in Phoenix, because his father had died when he was 14 and he could relate. The boy he was matched with was a kid from the Dupavilla Projects. He was a 2nd or 3rd generation welfare recipient. What Mike did for him was get him out to see what else was in the world and encourage him, because the boy didn't know anything but welfare."

"Then we moved here. I was pregnant, but wanted to do something, and a friend of mine, Cheryl Stewart, said the local Big Brothers needed someone to volunteer to do social work."

When Kathleen went to her first meeting it was a small group running a boys mentoring program and it wasn't even called Big Brothers/Big Sisters. Since it was just for boys it was Big Brothers. And since it was a small local effort it was not associated with the national organization to start with. It was started in 1971 by some locals who managed to arrange for a grant to fund some VISTA volunteers to help get it going. Local attorney Jim Musgrove was working for U.S. Senator and former Governor Paul Fannin at the time and helped secure the grant. Bill Murphy, no relation to Kathleen, was director of a boys club which he turned into an early Big Brothers program, and worked hard to build that up. Barbara Polk was another founder, and key in starting a number of good endeavors around town. They had VISTA volunteers in both Prescott and the Verde Valley and match kids in both areas.

Bill Murphy later resigned to take a job at the Police Department but continued as a board member. Two of the VISTA volunteers were a couple, Rob and Mary Ameln, who continued to be involved in the community for years after their work with Big Brothers. They built up a board of directors to oversee the organization. After the VISTA grants ran out the volunteer board ran the agency. One of the members of the board at that time was Bob Buchicchio who was the director of West Yavapai Guidance Clinic board.

By 1974, when Kathleen joined, the number of Bigs had fallen to about 14, and they had $649 in the bank. She volunteered to be a board member, reluctant secretary, and case manager. After a fund raising event they were able to hire her for 10 hours a week at a minimal rate as Executive Director and Case Manager.

"The thing I remember is we had these very caring people on the board but it was all volunteer, which meant it was unlikely to last. The VISTA volunteers, whom they had had for four years, reached the end of their contract. It became very clear that for the most part the people who were on the board who were good at wanting to do well by the kids, weren't the people who could move forward and raise funds."

"A restaurant in town did a fundraiser for us and that gave us the money to get started. They hired me for 10 hours a week at a small rate and then we began to look at how else to raise funds to keep the organization going. Fund raising scares most people. I suppose that's one place my upbringing helped because in the Catholic schools I went to we were always raising money for something."

After a year of going along with only a few new matches she received an important challenge from Barbara Polk who was still on the board. She had a good eye for where to put effort and where not to. Barbara said that while the boys program was good, it wasn't doing enough to be worth the effort and should be shut down, and the effort redirected to something else that worked better.

Kathleen was surprised at this. For one thing she thought that what good it was doing was worthwhile. For another, she felt this kind of program was crucial. From her experience working at the detention center she knew this was exactly what would keep boys out of the detention center. At the same time she realized Barbara had a point. Kathleen also probably got her stubbornness up. Never tell her she can't do something.

She asked Barbara to give it a year and see if it could grow. With renewed focus and sense of mission, she dove into making the agency and the number of children it served grow. She still had to do this part time, while being a mother and wife. But it was the start of her realizing that whether this organization made it, was up to her. It was her baby. She started to have a vision for the organization, a realization that it could grow much, much bigger and do a tremendous amount of good.

She was using space at the Guidance Clinic. At first whatever space was open, which was a step up from the original board meetings which were just in members homes. Later, thanks to Don Ostendorf, a small office in the clinic, which had previously been the furnace room, was set aside for the program. Don also joined the board that year.

She started to have a few more matches, and there were some fund raisers, and Bill Murphy helped her apply for grants. In 1979 they had 22 matches going, and they made their first contact with the national Big Brothers/Big Sisters organization to look into it. As part of looking into joining the national organization Kathleen when to her first national training session.

John

John, out of college, was continuing to work at the Franciscan Renewal Center called Casa. He applied to Catholic Social Services in Phoenix but they weren't hiring. They told him that the nun who was running Catholic Social Services in Prescott, Sister Sybil, was hiring. He applied with her and she had about six hours of interviews with him. This was in August. In October he saw her at Casa and she asked if he was still interested. He was, and she hired him. They moved to Prescott.

John was happy both for the job and because he had grandparents living here who he was attached to. Unfortunately the grandmother died a few days before they moved to Prescott, and the grandfather died a few weeks later.

There were a couple of other connections in Prescott that existed or were starting. One was that Max Bell was on the board of Catholic Social Services when John started. Another was that John's wife had gone to school with Kathleen Murphy. A third connection is that John's wife is a cousin of Brad Newman.

For the first several years CSS was a very small service, run by Sister Sybil.

Brad

Brad, 23 years old, having left his almost finished degree, was heading for Prescott and his new job. Before arriving in Prescott he called ahead to the rehab center to ask that a staff meeting be arranged. That first day he walked in the front door and was immediately confronted by one of the rehab patients who had heard that a man named Newman was coming to run the place. This patient grabbed Brad before he could speak to anyone else and was crying, "Mr. Newton, Mr. Newton, they want me to do work today and I don't want to work today, and the director lady is trying to make me and I can't because...". Brad said, "Okay let's go see the director lady and show me the job." The patient led him into the workshop and showed him the job and went on about how he didn't want to do the job assembling some parts that they had a contract to do. Brad said, "If you don't feel up to doing the job then maybe you need to go home today." The patient started a new cry about how he couldn't go home and his mother wouldn't understand. So Brad said, "Well maybe you should just sit down and do the job then." The worker, not knowing what else to do, sat down and started working. The director lady was favorably impressed. So in the first ninety seconds of his job Brad had made his first good impression.

Getting off to a good start felt especially good to him because he was nervous when he arrived for his first day.

Then he had the chance to go to the front desk and introduce himself and verify the staff meeting. The woman at the front desk confirmed his meeting and handed him a letter she had typed to Cypress Bagdad Mine thanking them for a donation they had made. He just had to sign it. He thanked her very much but explained that he could write his own thank you letter and that it might come out more personal that way. The receptionist was again impressed. She was used to the way things ran in offices in the 50s in which the boss would simply say, "Take a letter" or expect his staff to do routine letters for him. A boss who wrote his own letters was something new.

Next Brad asked the woman who was keeping the books to come into his office. He asked, "what is the cash flow, where does it come from and why, where does it go to and why?" He's still not sure where the term "cash flow" came from. It was not in his vocabulary at the time, and it's not a term he would have picked up in his studies since they had nothing to do with business.

He got a clear picture of the "cash flow" though. It was negative. A previous Christmas payroll had bounced. Insurance had been canceled for lack of payment. Some local citizens were organizing a lawsuit for mismanagement. Brad doesn't know the whole story of the man who was the previous director but gathers that there was some malfeasance involved. Yavapai Exceptional Industries (YEI, or actually YEI! as they use it, and pronounced "yee") was formed in 1974

Next the secretary informed him that a meeting to sign a continuation of the contract with the local school system for rehab services had been scheduled some time past, and he was due to go meet them shortly. Arriving there he met the man who ran special education services for the district. Brad's impression was that he was around retirement age. He couldn't have been more right. The first thing the man did was introduce Brad to a young man who was his replacement. His name was Marshall and, like Brad, has continued to work with challenged kids all these years. He and Brad became great friends and still are.

He shortly met with the board whom he had interviewed with for the job. When he had interviewed his dress and style were more that of a cowboy, which fit the local area fine. At his first day of work he showed up with shorter, neater hair and dress slacks and a jacket. The board kind of wondered if this guy was really going to fit what they needed.

He laid out three goals for them he wanted to accomplish in two years. One, own their own building, and own it outright so they wouldn't have rent or mortgage to pay. Two, become nationally accredited. Three, be financially sound, based largely on production; that is on the contract work the workers took in and the products they produced and sold.

Goals two and three, accreditation and earning significant income from production, were unusual. Accreditation in particular. The board was familiar with meeting state standards so that the state would pay them for each person they cared for. Accreditation, however, was something new and the board was not familiar with it. Brad had decided it would be an important piece of credibility and indication of quality for YEI to achieve. The board members were uncertain but impressed with this idea.

His start up experiences, continuing through the first couple of years, though, were a tough learning period for Brad. For one thing he was used to kids being at camp for a few weeks for fun. In that setting they had pretty fixed schedules for the whole group. They would, for instance, do archery from 8:00 to 10:00, then swimming till 12:00, then after lunch do crafts till 2:00, etc. He tried a similar schedule at YEI. He would schedule everyone to do mail sorting from 8:00 to 10:00, then assembly till 12:00, then after lunch do some volunteer work, etc. Unfortunately what he came to learn over time was that many of these people had a hard time shifting gears that precisely. If they were settled into mail sorting some of them were better off just focusing on that for the whole morning. There was also the type of work different members were suited to. Some did well sitting in the assembly room all day assembling widgets and chatting with the others, while some did better at jobs that kept them moving around more, like helping with yard cleanup someplace. His staff had some idea, from experience, that the strict schedules he tried to impose were not the best way to go, but they were too polite to make a point of it. Eventually he learned to listen to the workers and find the best situations and schedules that worked for various people.

Another mistake was to focus more on whether everyone was having fun rather than on productive work, and particularly on the quality of the work. He figured he would let his staff worry about production issues while he tried to make sure everyone was having a good time. With that in mind, in his first week, he decided the whole gang should take a walk down to the grounds of the courthouse square at lunch time. A great many people who worked in the downtown area ate their lunches on the courthouse grounds, and he was focused on his crew living normal lives and enjoying themselves, so it made sense to him that they should do the same. The idea of taking the whole crew there shocked some of his staff and frightened some of the parents. False starts like this made for some rough learning experiences. But Brad was not a quitter. He worked through the rough starts, and before long was well on the way to achieving those three goals.

He also didn't stop learning. He heard that there was a course being offered in Phoenix on the work of Wolf Wolfensberger,

Phd. who had developed the concept of "normalization" for developmentally challenged people. Prior to that time the emphasis was on institutionalization. For a while normalization became the guideline. Most of the rehab community has given up on normalization but to Brad it seemed that normalization should be the true goal. It was important enough to him to make the regular commute to take this class down in Phoenix and learn more about how to make normalization work. And he has made it work for his people.

MIDDLE YEARS

John

About four years into his work at Catholic Social Services Sister Sybil became the Diocesan Director, or CEO, of Catholic Social Services, which required her moving to Phoenix. John applied for her job as Executive Director of the Yavapai CSS. He says he thinks he was unqualified but that the board hired him anyway.

At that point there was a staff of about 15 people. Within three or four years they got several big grants for programs and were up to about sixty employees.

It was an incredible experience to go into the job "not knowing anything" and to become very adept at the facets of the job that he had to learn, and to become successful at those things. He says they were all team projects, so he didn't feel like he was accomplishing these things by himself. Some of the job facets he had to learn were budgeting and managing contracts.

He had never done a budget before. He did his first one, for about $250,000, for submission to Monseigneur Moyer who was the Diocesan liaison.

At that time such things were done by hand. Before long they were doing them on computer which was a big plus. What used to take three weeks could now be done in three days. If a change had to be made back at the beginning of the budget they used to have to carry corrections through the whole document. Now it all updated automatically.

John's telling of the story of the service during his time is mostly about the people. The ones who were wonderful to work with. The ones who have passed away. There were several personal tragedies among the people in his office or connected with it. Sister Sybil passed away some years later from complications of an operation. An employee's child was killed by a car, another's child drowned, the bookkeeper died at the office. All of these emotional losses pulled the staff together.

Some of the service he particularly enjoyed their being able to provide were child-protective type services, parent aid services, counseling services, and foster care work.

John and Joan had a foster child in the early eighties. Their foster daughter, Debra, came to them when she was in her mid-teens. She still lives in the area and they are quite close.

Of working in Prescott he says, "Being involved in Prescott has always been a real special place to be because all of us, certainly, were competitors from time to time, but we also knew each other. A lot of us personally knew each other, and so could provide a lot of support and caring for each other and that kind of thing. As time went on it got harder to do that, because of the competitive nature of that. It was sad because social services moved from people just kind of out doing good, to a business. The corporation I worked for probably has a $30 million dollar budget. If you screw that up, if you're off a percent, you have a lot of money to worry about at that point. So you had to be more cautious about that. But I always felt like the community was incredibly supportive of us. I thought the people who worked in that social services community, up until probably 5 or 6 years ago could be very supportive of each other, and real caring of each other, and respectful, and loving toward each other. Work with each other, help each other do things. Max was almost a founding member of the board of CSS, and he helped me restore the building we got." Max was also president of the board several times.

The building John is referring to was an important step in their progress. It is at 160 North Summit Avenue. As best they can tell from records it was built in 1886. When they got it in 1983 it hadn't been occupied since 1962. When John first went through it he thought they might have made a big mistake. But they renovated it and it was their main building for a long time.

In the course of a few years around this time several of the group moved to bigger, better facilities. In addition to CSS moving into this new building, Gordon moved juvenile services into a new center, Max move Child Protective Services into a new building, and Don moved the Guidance Clinic to a building on Cortez Street.

The building CSS bought had for years had been owned and lived in by Katherine Ready. When John got it there were old cars in the garage, one from 1939. There were six apartments in it and she had apparently lived in one at a time until care of that one got to be too much and then she would move into the next one. The doors of many rooms and apartments were nailed shut. When they cleaned it out they found many checks she had never cashed, old report cards from Saint Joseph's Academy that showed how bright she was. There were many old clawfoot bathtubs and wood burning stoves. They filled 72 wardrobe boxes with remnants found there. John later asked if she wanted to go through any of it before they got rid of it, but she didn't want to. The termite inspector wouldn't go into it because it was "haunted".

In 1962 she moved to another place just up the street. Over the next twenty years the unoccupied building was trashed by kids. Not a single unbroken window in it. Great leaks in the roof. Various doctors and others who wanted it for offices had tried to buy it. A couple of times it came within minutes of being sold for back taxes, but her lawyer, who was a friend of her family, would rush down and pay it.

What finally triggered her selling it was that John Olsen's wife (the owners of Olsen's Grain) played bridge with Katherine regularly. One day when Katherine was at their house John cornered her and told her that CSS wanted to buy it. John and his wife and Katherine were all tightly connected to the church. She agreed to sell it.

The only reason they had the funds to buy the building was because of what John calls Gene Polk's "good brain power". Gene's wife Barb had been on the board for years. The fund that Gene managed, the Yavapai County Community Foundation, had given one-half million dollars to CSS in Phoenix to buy a building to start a particular program there. He had put in the agreement a clause that if they ever sold that building a percentage had to come back to CSS in Prescott. With that they were able to buy the building for $60k.

John Olsen and Barbara Polk were also members of the CSS board when John was hired.

In a remarkably short time they renovated the building, between March and November, putting another $120k into it. All the staff helped out, stripping the seven layers of wall paper off and such. All of the electrical and plumbing had to be redone. Several walls had to be redone.

John and Max redid the staircase and doors, stripped them and redid them, a huge number of extra hours. John almost managed to burn the building down shortly after they got it. John and Max were using a stripping chemical and torches to take the old finish off of wood work. John managed to ignite a stretch of baseboard with flammable chemical on it so the whole stretch had four foot flames coming up off of it. Luckily he had put fire extinguishers in the building, so after he ran up the stairs to get them he was able to put it out.

"We moved in in November with no heat, Thanksgiving weekend. I certainly couldn't get by with that kind of stuff today, but in those days I could ask people to do crazy things and they would do it. Because they knew two things: That I would do whatever suffering needed to be done along with them. And they knew that I really cared about them so I would get that taken care of as fast as I could." He rounded up every space heater he could find until they could get the boiler working.

"Today you can't do that. People aren't as willing to do something like work in a building without heat."

"There were between 20 and 40 people then. In those days I knew everybody and their family members. Later we got to the point where someone would have to remind me who they were, which, from my perspective, is pretty silly. "

"I missed that part, as we got bigger, of having that real nice connection with people. As we got bigger, as I don't know them, they don't know me. So then they're not going to go work in a building without heat or whatever."

As part of John's focus on the people he knew along the way he remembers them in his prayers each day. People who were important to the work, or meant a lot to him. Many of whom have passed over the years. He has a long list he prays for each day.

"We could do all the work, all the daily stuff that needed to be done, but so much of what we did depended on having people in the community who really believe in us and what we were doing. People who were respected in the community who believed in us."

"We had a lot of fun and I really loved my work." They had a management consultant come in once. In the course of a seminar with them he asked each why they did what they did. "I told him because it was the one way I could implement my spiritual values into my daily life, and get paid for it."

"My style of leadership is what would be called a servant-leader. I'm here to make sure you have what you need to get what you need done."

In addition to growing in number of employees, the paperwork also grew. "When I started as a licensed professional counselor my entire case record was on a set of 5x7 cards. I would keep session notes on the back. When you go from 'our purpose is serving people' to 'our purpose is serving people but you've got to do a whole lot of stuff so you can prove you did what you say you're doing'. And you have to show that all your interventions are based on research oriented methods. When that's the focus, people get cranky. We're telling them 'we have this impossible number of people for you to see, and by the way, you have to be perfect in your documentation, and you're going to be reviewed on it many times.'"

The paperwork requirements grew over time to the point that in senior staff meetings John would remind them that "our main purpose is to help people". It gave them a lot of support to know that he knew that, and that he wanted them doing what they love to do.

Of his own counseling he says, "I was surprisingly an adequate counselor. Sister Maggie who had been around for a while told me that I was a really good counselor that could handle difficult problems. Father Berry at the Franciscan Renewal Center had a waiting list of people waiting for his counseling. He told me he would rather send a difficult case to me than to a counselor we both knew who was well known and had written numerous books on counseling. That really surprised me. It gave me some confidence that maybe I could be okay at it. Whenever I have been working with kids I've had very good success. It's not that I'm such a great counselor but what they get from me is how much I care about them, that I really like them."

As director he had to do a lot of public relations work. "Another thing I had to become better at, I would never say I was good at it, was doing presentations in public, or speaking at the gala balls, or doing training. I started out petrified, but got to the point where I just accept my inadequacies and just go out and do it anyway."

What he enjoyed more was providing as many services as possible to as many people as possible. "Our services were very diverse. Emergency services, weatherizing homes, we had carpenters working for us to do those kinds of things. We had a transitional shelter. Around 1985 we started and were only one of two programs in the state for treatment of sexually abused kids. We did a program in later years called New Responses which provided counseling services to the four most difficult problems to deal with in kids, oppositional defiance disorder, reactive attachment disorder, sexually reactive disorder, and attention deficit/hyper active disorder. Imagine someone funding a program where success is considered 25 percent of the kids improve. We managed to beat that goal. With all those different services going I remember one year we served 23,000 people."

"We also had services for the elderly going from the beginning. Right at the beginning of my time there, there was a lady named Ann Marie Lopez who had done a door-to-door assessment in town of what kind of services elderly people needed. Her canvassing was really amazing. That became one of our bigger programs."

"We were doing well over 15,000 hours of service in the homes of elderly. We had networks set up so they could call each other make sure they were alive that morning. We did housekeeping, home health-aide services and visiting nurse services. We did an advocate for the disabled program that helped people who had been denied Social Security Disability. That went on for some years until some attorneys started to get interested because there was some profit in it. You'll see that on television now."

"Some of those stories were just incredible. We had cases of someone living in a cave, and our worker would go out and visit them in the cave. Of course they didn't have any of the documentation they needed. We would get psychiatrists and doctors to document their disabilities. Emergency services was huge, we would serve thousands of people every year providing food and emergency shelter. Transitional shelter probably came in in the mid 1980s. We used to put people up at the Vendome Hotel and the Hassayampa Hotel before it was redone. Sacred Heart Church had a fund that helped us with that. This was before the days when the state started putting money into utility assistance and transitional housing and such. We had to hustle up all those funds."

"We did a huge amount of foster care. When I left we had 330 foster homes in Northern Arizona and they were all run out of Prescott. Prescott became the hub for CSS for Northern Arizona. Our office was bigger than the Phoenix office. Sybil asked me at one time to help run the Mesa office for a while. I helped open the Mojave office, opened the Cottonwood office."

Maintaining funding was always part of his job. "It took a lot of connection with funding sources. I had an approach that they found real appealing, I would do whatever they wanted. Whatever they wanted to fund. They were the customer. My outlook is not that the client is the customer. I thought of the client as our product. If we could help someone get on their feet, get a job, that was a successful outcome. Whoever funded that, my job was to keep them happy, to make sure we were doing what they wanted us to do."

The funding for all this did not come from the Catholic Church. John would frequently do presentations trying to get support, and the question would come up of how much the church funded. It only funded about 3 percent of their budget. He would use that money as match money to get government funding and other grants.

"We also just did a lot ourselves. One time we had to get a huge load of new office furniture. We had people in Child Protective Services offices around the state, in cases where that's what made the most sense for the job some staff member was doing. We got furniture for a bunch of these offices. I just rented a truck and loaded it up and hauled it up to Flagstaff. The various office managers would meet me there and get their furniture and haul it to their offices. I did that several times. I think that is probably true of a lot of us that have done this. That you just do what needed doing. I didn't hire a guy to go do it. I did it because I knew I wanted them to realize where that came from. So I was there helping them load their desks and such and they would think, maybe John's a pretty good guy to have a contract with, because he's not going to be a prima donna. I'd clean the bathrooms when the janitor was on vacation and do things like that."

Max

Max was now supervisor of CPS for all of Yavapai County. He talks about how the agency matured over time. "I think the agency just got better and better at child abuse issues. Training got more and more focused. The training being offered to CPS workers was being more developed. When I first started our core training was three days and then we could do CPS investigations. That's now turned into a number of weeks over a long period of time and it's experience based. You get a week of training, then go back to your office and do some on the job stuff, and then you go back for another week. I think it is six weeks long. It's called CPS Academy. They go over all kinds of issues in that training. Cultural issues, in depth of what to look for, how to assess risk, how to actually conduct the investigation, how to coordinate with police departments."

CPS is an agency that naturally has a lot of overlap with other social service and law enforcement functions. That has led to it focusing more on its core function and some of the support services being picked up more by other agencies. Also growth of the area meant eventually Cottonwood, and later Prescott Valley needed to lead their own CPS offices, which allowed Max to focus on Prescott.

One of the agencies they overlapped with was Catholic Social Services. CPS did a lot of work with CSS. When we first started we had a foster home licensing worker. That's now done by other agencies. CSS did a lot of that for us. Arizona Children's Association which used to be called Arizona Children's Home did a lot. A lot of times the private agencies will do foster home licensing, and recruitment, and training. Those are things CPS used to do that they no longer do. When I first started we also had a lot to do with child care, day care. That's now a separate department under the Department of Economic Security."

At the same time CPS developed more specialists. "It used to be we'd investigate all different kinds of abuse and neglect, and now some CPS offices have specialists in sex abuse. I had a worker who I assigned all of the baby cases because she was so good at them. I had a couple of workers who were really adept at working with teenagers and so they work entirely with them, because teenagers have their own set of issues. Baby cases are considered really high risk, so you do need people who really know what they're doing. If you have a failure to thrive case or a drug exposed baby case, you really need someone who's had experience, who's had training, who knows what to look for, to deal with those kinds of special issues. I had one worker who could just tell by the feel of the baby's weight if the baby was potentially a failure to thrive case. What it felt like and looked like, the skin color. Some of the workers would have no idea what to look for."

Another organization they overlapped with was CASA, the Court Appointed Special Advocacy program. It is another organization that Barbara Polk was involved in starting. "CASA is completely different. CASA is run right from the courts and they are only responsible to the court."

"The way the CASA program works is when CPS removes a child, they place that child in foster care and file a dependency petition with the juvenile court. When that case moves through court, the court can order that a CASA worker be appointed to represent the child right from the git-go. That CASA is only responsible to the court. CASA has no connection to CPS. So if the CASA believes CPS should do certain things they will recommend that in their report. Their responsibility is just to advocate for the child. They don't care about budget problems or other problems that agencies might have. I found them to be very effective at advocating for the child. I can remember a couple of cases where we felt we needed to sever the rights of the parents. The parents were fighting that. If the CASA agrees with us it adds credibility to the recommendation."

CASA is one of the reviews and double checks children in the system get. "Kids in foster care get several objective reviews. In addition to CASA and the judge himself, there's the Foster Care Review Board. All cases that are in foster care, every six months, get reviewed extensively by a panel of citizens and they report directly to the court."

Max worked with a number of judges over the time. "Judge Brutinel is the presiding judge over CASA. He's also still the juvenile judge. Judge Brutinel is always doing creative, innovative things (the Juvenile Justice Court being one). He's a good judge, real thoughtful, careful. That's a tough job too."

"Judge Rosenblatt was the first judge I worked with. He got appointed to the federal court. The I worked with Judge Hancock. Then he retired and I worked with Judge Sult. Then he got appointed to the appeals court, and since then I've work with Judge Brutinel."

Since then Judge Brutinel has become Justice Brutinel of the Arizona Supreme Court.

Another agency they work with is the Family Advocacy Center. "Now they have the Family Advocacy Center in Prescott Valley that's a real helpful tool to CPS that I didn't have when I first started. They will even do a complete screening of a child who may have been physically or sexually abused. It can be taped and they can bring in a specially trained doctor, and have nurses on hand who have been trained in what to look for. The County Attorney's office is also involved. So right from the git-go you can have a coordinated case with law enforcement, CPS, and mental health. What's good about that is the child has a minimum number of interviews. Law enforcement likes it because they want the best quality out of those interviews. No leading the child. You don't want a case thrown out because of a bad interview, which has happened. Becky Ruffner started that. Kathy McLaughlin is in charge of that and she worked for years at the sheriff's department so she knows what kind of activities need to occur."

The cooperation between CPS and other agencies came to be know state wide. "I think Prescott has always been—at least it always was when I was working—we always had a reputation for doing pretty good in terms of inter-relationships between agencies and working together. I can remember hearing from people like supervisors from Flagstaff or other communities, they never could get past the turf issues and the ability to work together, to coordinate activities, coordinate case plans, coordinate services for clients. Having joint staffings and actually being able to come up with some kind of a cooperative plan as a result of the joint staffing."

That paid off for Prescott CPS once. There was some money available for an agency to put together an MDT, a Multi-Disciplinary Team, to coordinate services and needs in a case. The Maricopa agency would have been first in line but they couldn't pull such a group together. So they called up Max because of the reputation here for coordination. Here again, Becky Ruffner plays a role. "We were the first CPS in the state to have an effective MDT. We got the funding to put ours together because Maricopa at that time couldn't put together an MDT, so the funding went to us. I called up Becky Ruffner and asked her if she could help us put that team together."

"That was 15 or 20 years ago. They had existed in other states but it was kind of new to Arizona. We had a team of 12 community professional people, and when CPS had a tough case we could have MDT review the case. Chick Hastings, when he was County Attorney, he was on it. Pediatrician Dr. Mick was on it. Usually somebody from the Guidance Clinic. The MDT team could make recommendations on coordination. Things like services to the family."

"Another goal was effective prosecution. There would be cases where we would remove a child from a home but they may not have a good criminal case. Sexual abuse cases could be that way if the child had a consistent story of abuse but there were no witnesses. Sometimes that couldn't be prosecuted. When you remove a child there's a different standard of evidence. For the criminal prosecution the standard may be beyond a reasonable doubt. For removing the child the standard was what the preponderance of evidence indicated."

CPS also overlapped with the juvenile legal system and with the Guidance Clinic. "A lot of our kids were involved in 'juvie'. A lot were involved in mental health issues. One time Gordon and I did a study on our own. We looked at our lists of kids to see how many of them that were in juvie had a history with CPS. We were amazed at how many did. In some cases it may not be the child in juvenile trouble now who had been reported abused, but maybe an older brother a few years earlier had been."

"A lot of our kids were getting mental health services from the Guidance Clinic. Don and I would talk a lot about how to work out problems. Gordon and I would talk a lot. With a lot of these kids it was hard to tell if they were dependent minors or delinquent minors. And you really needed to work that out. Sometimes there would be a dual adjudication, for dependency and delinquency. I don't see why kids couldn't be on probation but in foster care. That way if the kid commits a criminal act while they're in foster care, and have violated their probation, then the criminal system can take over. But if they don't, then they can be in foster care. I think there needs to be more of that."

The cooperation helped with effective use of funding among the various agencies. "Funding has always been an issue because DES only has a certain amount for foster care, the juvenile court only has a certain amount of money for foster care, the Guidance Clinic only has a certain amount for residential treatment. All three of those systems are usually under-funded. Those kinds of residential treatments or placing with foster care are very expensive, but yet it still needs to be done."

One thing was constant, the second-guessing by the public. "I hated calls from reporters because the family, or others in the community, could make whatever comments they wanted about some case, but because of confidentiality rules we couldn't state our side. I remember a case where the family was telling everyone the child shouldn't have been taken away because it was all about the child having one fractured bone. What we couldn't say was that there had been many other bone fractures in the past. But we had to tell the press we couldn't say anything because of confidentiality, and then they would accuse us of hiding behind that. So that was frustrating."

Don

Don's sequence of jobs had finally led to the West Yavapai Guidance Clinic in Prescott. "When I started we were in the what is the County Annex building on Marina. I had eight or ten staff. The volume and pace of the work was much less then."

"It felt like a small town. There was one pizza parlor and no fast food chains. Abia Judd was on our board, as was Judge Rosenblatt, and Lindsay Bell and Jean Phillips. My wife and I thought we would be here a few years and move on, and here we are all these years later."

"Prescott would be way to big for me today if I hadn't grown with it. If it had been this big when I came here I would have turned around and run the other way. "

That played a role in how each of the group of six operated, and how they operated together. "I think this is a connection to the others in this group, is that we made it a small town. We kept it a small town as long as we could. Even now, we're all friends. What makes this group so unique, is that the principle players in social services in this town are in that group. We had this social service thing covered. So we relied on each other, we were friendly. We showed up at the same places and could call up on a Friday and say let's go have some coffee. And we'd set every thing aside and just go bullshit for a while. Maybe do a little business, but mostly just stay connected. Maybe try to work out a problem informally before it became something that could find its way to another level. You were protecting what you had, and you did that by helping the other people. That skill I think was kind of a natural strategy for all of us. There was a bond there of some kind that was pretty special even early on."

As time went along the clinic grew. "The growth of the clinic just kind of pulled you along. The community kept growing and growing. If you're going to be the provider you'd better grow with it."

"All of that is different now because of competition in health care. That may or may not be true for the other five, but it's certainly true in health care. Back in the 70s and 80s there was no competition because nobody wanted to do mental health work. Part of the reason I left is because now it's competitive. There are people who want that business. They think they can do it better or less expensively. But at the time growth just went with the territory. The town gets bigger, more services are needed, nobody else is going to do it, so we do it."

"So you are the only shop in town, which can be good because you have a monopoly, and can be bad because you have a monopoly. You get the credit for your successes, but you get all the criticism for your failures. There wasn't much chance to do things poorly because we were a monopoly, because the community would deal with that. In a big city you can kind of hide. The patient who's unhappy, the family who thinks they were mistreated, they'll go somewhere else. Or you can send them somewhere else. Not here."

"A lot of the anecdotes I can think of about the work are related to that. They were cases where nobody else is going to do it, and it's happening, so we're going to have to take care of it, somehow."

"There was a case of someone in one of the nicer neighborhoods shooting off a rifle, on a weekend. A SWAT team had a stand-off with him but managed to coral him. They put him in jail, but within hours he paid his bond and got out. He had a lot of money. So the cops thought, 'Now what are we going to do'. So they followed him and he went right back to a bar and started drinking again. So the chief called me at home and said, 'Don, we need a favor'. I called one of our psychiatrists. We went down to the office and found we had dealt with this guy once before and could build a little case to commit him under the civil commitment statute, and the doctor has the authority under law to do that. But it was a bit of a stretch because we were operating on second hand information from the police, and the fear that he could do something worse, and under the law, alcohol alone is not enough reason. But we got it done. The doc issued the order, the police picked him up and held him."

"There were any number of times where we would work with, if not the police, then Max Bell or John Allen and put something together that was good for the patient and the community but called for a little imagination or bending the rules or figuring out the best way to salvage it."

There was a lot of learning how to grow along the way. "I wasn't living in isolation here. Part of my job was to look around and see how other communities have dealt with growth. There was an era that was really very exciting where, with the help of our regional mental health administrator group, we traveled all over the country and look at how to provide in-patient services for our size. That directly led to the opening of the Hillside facility. We went to three or four communities in Utah, to Sacramento, some of the California rural areas like Lodi, and we brought back those ideas and put them into place. The administrators' group was administrators from places like ShowLow and Flagstaff and Kingman. We would go off on a mission to study this stuff."

Even as it grew, there was still a small town way of going about things. "Another example, and demonstrates maybe the last example of the, 'we're all here together stuck with a problem, let's all get together and try to figure something out', was what became the Mile Stones Project. Gordon and I were serving on a public safety advisory committee at the city. That was going on when the Columbine High School mass shooting happened. Gordon was on that committee and I remember a conversation where we said, 'let's face it, that could happen here'. That led to a network that in theory would prevent a similar situation. That happened because of an acknowledgment that it wasn't the problem of any one of us but it involved all of us. And yes we didn't have any money but we still needed to get it done somehow."

"We got everybody together, including the school systems, over at Dexter school, and Carl Brown with Youth Count was very helpful in this, and we came up with a model that worked well. We intercepted a heck of a lot of kids. We started with the idea that the kids who did the shooting at Columbine were known to the system, but the system wasn't talking to each other. In that case the police had dealt with them, the school knew they had problems, the parents knew something was wrong, but they didn't put it together. We asked ourselves how we could be on alert, and if we detected something, validate that concern through this network."

"That seemed pretty easy until you ran into some of the lawyers and they said, 'confidentiality'. But again, it's a small town. When you have the Superior Court judge and the County Attorney at the table, you begin to find your way through that, when in another place you might just give up. We took the approach that there was enough protection in the civil statutes about 'duty to warn' and such, and kept the information basic, that it would be okay. So if for example, some kid had shot his sister with a BB gun we could check to see if any other agency had information about this kid that might indicate that there might be more to this problem."

"So we empowered each member of the group to call a meeting whenever there was an issue to discuss, and the obligation was you had to show up. The key was in getting the parents' consent, who were, more often than not, starved for help. So it might be the principal who would approach the parent and say we are concerned about their kid. Often the parents were concerned too, and then the principal could tell them we might be able to help. Then we can pull together people from the juvenile program, the Guidance Clinic and maybe the school counselor and offer some help."

Keeping all that small town approach working took a lot of people skills. "One thing you need for this kind of service in a small growing community is the ability to bring the community along with you. The people skills and such that allow people to invest in the mission and be a genuine partner with you. I was able to be pretty savvy at that, and I attribute some of that to growing up in Addieville, Illinois because you'd better be able to get along with just about everybody. It's different now because it's so competitive. A health care administrator has to have those same people skills, but he also has to be a really tough business person to not let competition move into the territory. But those people skills and an ability to earn respect in a variety of settings were key."

"And the willingness to do it. I've known every legislator in this area because you need to engage those people and let them know what your successes are, what your needs are. I played volleyball with Ken Bennett (state senator and Secretary of State) in the old days. Even now I need to know when to call him Ken and when to call him Senator Bennett, and who I might open his door to, and I'm very selective about that. Similarly I kept John Hays (state senator) informed of what we were doing."

And it also took political skill. "In this state money starts in Phoenix, and by the time it gets here it may not be as well suited to what the perceived needs were in Phoenix. So another part of the savvy is how to adapt the services so they meet the expectations of Phoenix, but also meet the needs of a smaller area. And that's an ongoing challenge that Max and Gordon and others all have to take account of. For instance Phoenix tells us they've studied the meth problem and here's the service you need to provide to deal with it. And it might work in central Prescott, but it won't in Chino Valley, or in Ash Fork. How do you navigate that? You've got to somehow adapt it, stay within the rules, but still meet the local needs."

Learning new ways of improving the services was on ongoing process. "The six people in this group, there's this investment in the community; there's also an investment in trying to be on the edge of what's working in other places, so you can be gauging one against the other and try to make the best out of what's out there. So you don't isolate yourself, but on the other hand you stay invested locally."

"Gordon was a master at that. He was very invested in the area, but he was very connected with people at the state level. He mixed it up with people running programs all over the state, sometimes the country. Kathy is great at that too. She gets around the country. Yes she's delivering success stories locally but she's also taking in a wider perspective. I was good at that too, always on the prowl for an idea I could steal. The staff use to tease me about it, that when I went off to a conference they knew I would come back with ideas that they would have to implement. I'm more of an idea guy and a starter. I have to rely on other people for the longer term. I'm not much of a risk taker, but I am creative. Not business risks, which suited the community since it's kind of a conservative community."

"Just recently the MATForce program (Meth Amphetamine Task Force) started up. That came about after Judge Brutinel and I had a discussion about trying to build a better service relationship between the Courts and the Guidance Clinic. I made a pitch to him that not only was the town growing, we kept dealing with the same groups of people with problems, dealing with limited resources. Also we had some new players. Sheila Polk was relatively new as County Attorney, we had a new sheriff. Maybe we ought to all get together and have some better ideas of how to shape the system for down the line. He liked the idea and talked to Sheila. She liked the idea but wanted to focus on meth because it was such a problem. That's the way that started."

Marketing and fund raising were also essential skills. "Part of my style is, most public mental health centers do very little fund raising, marketing, promotion. They take what comes, advertise their service as being available, but they don't spend a lot of time marketing or trying to educate the community. That's something I did. That's what WYGC does now. Columns in the paper, fund raisers, and such, that I started. In my view we need to be proactive in shaping our image. Not allow the community to define us as just a place where poor people go to get services."

"Fund raising was also important because if you accept money from the community then you set the bar higher for yourself because you're more accountable locally. If you accept a dollar from someone and say it's important and we'll put it to good use, then you damn well better do it, and be able to show how you do it. The local donations are probably only 2 percent of our budget, but it says something to me, it says something about the organization."

Gordon

Juvenile Probation had moved into their new facility on Division Street. "We had our own detention center then. Shortly thereafter, we hired a couple more probation officers. The detention center was staffed by husband and wife teams, we called Houseparents. There were two teams. They would work two weeks straight and have two weeks off. They had an apartment there and they lived there for the two weeks. We usually just had a couple of kids at a time then. They could handle that, and it was more like a family environment. We didn't want it to be like an institution. We wanted it to be conducive to family and reality. We let families visit with the kids in a room where they could have contact, hug each other and be close to each other rather than visit them behind bars or a glass window. It's still that way today. It was important to us. It was some compromise of safety because they could pass things, but it was more important that the relationships and the environment was not so hard, that kids could grow there, and learn. That their time wasn't just stagnant."

"Through the years we were able to initiate some programs and an educational tutoring program in detention. Our goal was to make these youngsters a little better when they left than when they came in."

"We had an exercise yard where a kid could get out for at least an hour a day. We gradually got school in to them. They have a full fledged school now, which is fully computerized, a number of programs, and contracted counselors to come in. The detention officers take part in the programs with the kids.

They don't wear uniforms. In adult detention the officers mostly move inmates from place to place. There's not a lot of positive interaction. We like our detention officers to interact, give encouragement, advice, and take much more of an active role in the kid's stay there."

"We gradually went from house parents to round-the-clock staff in the 80s. As we grew, there were just more kids than a husband and wife could handle."

"In 1974 the legislature came up with the Family Counseling act, and they would allocate some money to probation departments to provide counseling. It wasn't much, and the county had to match 25% of it, but that's still going today. Still not much, but it was the first program fund in Arizona for juveniles. That started us on program development. I became the grant writer and the program developer. I wrote a lot of state and federal grant applications and was very successful in getting a lot of outside money to develop our programs for kids."

"One program I was very proud of that we got 25 years ago was an employment program. We focused on hands-on jobs that kids needed to know in order to make it. We wanted to have some way to teach them how to work and get them some money at the same time, for encouragement and to pay restitution. We'd put them to work at non-profit agencies for minimum wage, but rather than give them the money it went to restitution to repay their victims. Once they fulfilled their restitution order, they could start keeping the money. Later to add to the encouragement we let them keep 25% while they made restitution. If they owed community service hours, rather than just going out on a work crew they could go to these same non-profit agencies and get credit for that and get some real job experience. The program was evaluated a number of times and it was highly successful. Some of the youngsters would get hired by the agency they worked with and end up with long-term jobs."

"A lot of our programs were geared toward improving self-esteem and self-image. They became real member of society, contributing, working at it. So we tried to give them another option besides doing the stuff they shouldn't be doing. Something to lose, also. They were proud of their work and knew if they went down their old path they would lose it."

"We started a whole host of programs and resource opportunities for kids and families. That's one of my proudest accomplishments, going from very little to bringing us into the era of all these programs and resources. Yavapai county became a very highly respected county among our peers, state wide. If we could do an evaluation of a kid and their family when they first came in, and plug them into the right resources, they won't come back."

"We had a lot of emphasis on rehabilitation. We had a number of kids who had dysfunctional families who just were not willing to change. So with these kids our focus had to be on helping them make it in spite of their family and home environment."

"We also tried to keep kids at home with their families rather than placing them in foster care or elsewhere. It was much more successful to provide the assistance, support and structure to the families rather than removing the youngster from the home. But sometimes it was necessary to place them into foster care. If that wouldn't work, then we'd use a residential treatment program, like a boys or girls home. Not a state institution, a private one. We avoided that when we could because they were expensive, $3,000 to $6,000 a month, and were minimally effective."

"It became a very expensive baby-sitting or warehousing service, and we weren't getting the results. The kids would do well there but then fail when they got home. The families were in Prescott but most of these places were in Phoenix or Tucson. There was little coordination with families and our families couldn't get down there for family counseling and to develop an after-care plan. It just wasn't money well spent. So we tried to use our limited funds on the array of programs and resources locally so we could make it work here rather than shipping them away."

"If the kid still posed a risk and continued re-offending, the next step was the Department of Juvenile Corrections, the state institution in Phoenix. Once we sent kids there, we lose jurisdiction. They become a ward of the state, and the state determines how long they're going to stay, and where they're going to come back to. Even if they come back to this area they answer to a state parole officer, rather than to our department."

On the number of kids on psychiatric drugs, "We had a lot of kids on psychiatric drugs prescribed by doctors before they ever came to us. Some kids need that, but it's over used in my opinion. It creates an artificial environment for these kids and they don't learn through it."

He likes the results of some of their programs better: "One of the later programs was CJJC." (Community Juvenile Justice Committee). A first or maybe second time offender could be sent to this alternative program. The juvenile and parent would sit down with several community members who would interview him and decide whether he's a good candidate for some alternative program, like doing some community service work, paying restitution, and such. They might either meet with, or write to, the victims so they realize the effects of their crime. Having this done by a community members, rather than facing a judge, was intended to give the kid the effect of facing people who were neighbors and give them the feeling the community wanted to see them change course, and help them to do that.

"That approach just made sense to us. It kind of developed in part from my experiences growing up in Prescott. It was a small town then, and everybody knew everybody. I couldn't get away with squat. Before I got home, if I was doing something I shouldn't be doing, my folks would already know about it. Or some neighbors would step up and correct the problem. That's gone a lot now. So we tried to reinvent that with CJJC. The meetings with the kids would be held at community centers or other places away from our offices so it felt more like the community stepping in."

"We provided a lot of family counseling, but probably our best successes were in these concrete programs, or in getting them job skills."

Kathleen

Over the next few years the number of matches grew, the organization grew, and additional financing was found. For several years there was financial help from Office of Juvenile Justice. That helped them make the jump to officially joining the nationwide network of Big Brothers/Big Sisters, and start the Big Sisters part of the program. That financing ended after several years though, and ever since it has been mostly charitable fund raising and some grants that has kept it going.

Jim Musgrove helped on a couple of occasions by recommending BBBS to his clients who were planning their future finances. Two of his clients bequeathed sizable gifts to the agency in their estates.

Sometimes the budget was just barely making it though. Local businessman Rowle Simmons, who later became mayor, was on the board in the early 80s and can remember loaning money to make payroll for the small group of employees on a couple of occasions.

A contract with the Juvenile Detention Center, Gordon's agency, funds juveniles who come to them through that connection. They have had a very high rate of success with the children from the juvenile program.

In the following years they added programs for couples to be matched to kids, and for high school students to serve as Bigs, which also gets the high school students involved in volunteering. A later program is aimed at matching the children of parents in prison.

A key fund raiser, started by Paul Murphy, that developed over years is their Dinner and Auction. Brad Newman, who is a Big Brother himself, served as auctioneer a number of years. He was famous for wearing red tennis shoes when in a tuxedo. One year, having run out of things to auction, on a humorous lark befitting Brad, he auctioned off one of his shoes. Rowle Simmons got into a bidding war for it with local realtor Fred Lindquist, and Rowle won it. He later had the idea to bronze it and mount it on a plaque with room for many names to be listed on it, and only keep it for a year. It would be re-auctioned each year and be dubbed "The Great Sole Society". Over those years it has raised many thousands of dollars and it became something of a point of pride for locals to get their name on that plaque. Some of those who have won it include Patti & John Bennan, MD, Suzy & Ron Moore, DDS, Malcolm & Susan Barrett, Jr., Dino Bulleri, Marsha & Taylor Hicks, Jr., Nick Moceri & Margie Tays, Tonia Fortner, Sylvia Fann, Fred York, Matt Frankel, Don & Susie Hecht and Tony Booker.

Though they had been serving the entire county, they finally established an office in Cottonwood in 1986. In 1994 they decided they needed a more local connection to Prescott Valley and opened an office there. In 2008 they were able to move into their own building, made possible partly by John and Jason Gissi donating the site for it. Many donations were made toward the building, with Don and Shirl Pence pledging a major donation over time toward it. The building was named in their honor. The Pences helped again later by moving their pledge up to pay off the mortgage on the building. The intention being that future contributions can go to helping kids and not to making payments on a mortgage, which now enables the agency to fund many more matches. There is a parallel here in that both Brad and Kathleen find it a high priority to not have their organizations burdened with a mortgage.

While Kathleen was driving and managing all of this growth she was diligently focused on effectiveness and accountability. She was sure there were other BBBS agencies around the country who already knew how to do various aspects of the job well and she wanted to find out who, and what it was that they knew. As soon as she started to look into it, though, she found that the data was a little fuzzy. This started her on a parallel adventure of getting involved at the national level, creating some controversy, and ultimately, together with other concerned BBBS leaders, making big improvements at the national level, and ending up with the local organization being one of the best in the country.

"I had the sense to know that there were people who knew how to do it well so rather than doing the same thing over and over it seemed sensible to me to look out into the BBBS world and see who was doing it well. But you couldn't tell who was most successful because, maybe one agency was raising a lot of money, and some other agency was matching so many kids, but nobody knew how that compared to the size of the population they were serving. No one could say, 'Here's the size of my community and here's my degree of success within that community.' To me, because of my background in sociology and social science, and also from practical business sense, if you didn't know what portion of the kids you served or how much money you were raising in a given population, how do you know whether you were successful? So my first entry into the national level was beginning to get information from National that would answer those questions."

The "National" organization, BBBS of America, is, appropriately, in the city of brotherly love, Philadelphia. It sets basic standards and provides assistance to local, officially associated, BBBS agencies. Those agencies, like Yavapai BBBS (YBBBS), are independent agencies.

"We did have some information about how many kids were being served, but not relative to population. We knew how many kids were matched in a community, and how big the general population was, but not how big the population was of kids who might need a Big. I began to gather that information. At first they didn't have that. You just had to go in and ask questions and do research. So I began to gather that information and put it together. By doing that I could tell which agencies were the most successful. And then you had to look at other factors, like did they do good work?"

As soon as she started asking these questions and trying to gather this information she ran into resistance. "The problem with that was it went against the grain of the national organization. People said you can't talk about numbers, you just do good work. If you try to do it for too many kids it won't work." She finds in social service that a lot of people are well intentioned and many try hard, but some aren't up to the challenge of whether their efforts are, for instance, reaching a reasonable amount of the population of kids in need at a reasonable cost.

She also found resistance to her, as a woman, asking difficult questions. "There was a lot of major push-back. Especially from men. You're working with that cusp of men who are in their 60s now, who were born in the 40s and early 50s, prior to when the feminine revolution hit while we were all in college. Some men became more comfortable with that, and some didn't. There was tremendous push back on the part of people not wanting to be held accountable. That it didn't matter. It didn't matter how many kids they were serving. It didn't matter how big their community was, they didn't want to talk about it."

"Some weren't doing very good work. They weren't matching very many kids. Others who were doing good work or weren't afraid to look at the data were very interested in it. There was an agency in a major city that was spending a million dollars and only had 100 matches. They were only matching about one tenth as many kids for the size of their budget as we were. So there had been no accountability."

There were a couple of moments of major change in this story. One had to do with a meeting of the Executive Directors Association. This was an independent group, at that time recently formed, by directors of agencies around the country. For some it was just a group to get together with. For others who wanted to improve things it was a necessary independent group to push for change. Kathleen joined it. "Before that there was an organization supposedly of the people from the field but it was totally overwhelmed by the national staff. So you went to these meetings and sat there and listened to the national staff talk to you. So this was a grass roots association."

At one of the association meetings she attempted to present the data she had gathered. "I did all this research on percentage of kids being served in relationship to population, and I brought all the research to this meeting. One of the men from one of the Midwest agencies didn't want me to present it. He said, 'That's a really nice dress you have on, and we're really glad you got dressed up today but this has nothing to do with the Executive Directors Association.' I said, 'That's your opinion, and we're a body of people who each has a vote. So let's just

take a vote and see who wants to hear this and who doesn't.'"
The vote passed in favor of hearing the information.

"That night I took the dress and put it in a box and wrapped a ribbon around it. I handed it to him at the meeting the next morning. He opened it, and I said, 'Since you liked the dress so much I thought I'd give it to you.'"

Another crucial point came a little later. As the Executive Directors Association pushed for change, the national organization was resisting and ignoring them. In the meantime Kathleen had been elected president of the association. During this time Lynn Swann had become president of the National organization. Yes, the same Lynn Swann who was the SuperBowl winning, Hall of Fame, pro-football player. He liked the changes the Executive Directors Association was pushing and at one of their annual national meetings he invited Kathleen to attend and to sit next to him on the dais. This symbolic gesture reflected what was happening. Those resistant to the changes toward greater accountability were being overruled, and some of the changes being advocated were being adopted. Lynn continued for several years to be very involved in helping the organization improve.

As the national organization started to look at these methods Kathleen got a local board member, Ralph Weiger, to go talk to them. Ralph had headed up the Jiffy Lube national chain during its growth. "Ralph Weiger went and talked to them. He had come on our board. He had run Jiffy Lube and he had that same formula. Jiffy Lube would go in and look at how many people lived in a certain community, they'd figure out other factors, and then they knew how many Jiffy Lubes to put in that area so that they could have an outcome that they wanted."

"They also had contests to see who could lube a car the fastest and they would video them. Then they would get the ones who won and they would use those best practices and teach everybody those. Those two concepts, to me, were what the organization nationally needed, and what we needed. Ralph went and spent time with Tom McKenna (who was CEO of the National organization) to talk about these principles."

Some of the changes have remained over the years and some have slipped. The Executive Directors Association, having served its purpose, eventually disbanded. "Now they have the National Leadership Council which is led by volunteers and board members from agencies. So that somewhat fills that role. It's not as provocative and edgy as the association was but they've done a good job, they look at things. They're in charge of the program quality."

A third important step was when the local YBBBS collaborated with Harvard University on detailed studies of mentoring. In 1994 Kathleen was pursuing a grant for a new program from the Arizona Community Foundation. She knew being able to document results was important in grant programs, and she wanted the program to be maximally effective. "I wanted a business piece in there. I wanted to know how businesses do things." She knew local business woman and adventurer Molly McGinn was the person to talk to. Molly coached Fortune 500 companies around the world on executive performance, and as part of that did a lot of work with focus groups. Molly helped Kathleen with some focus groups connected with this program. The company that did the focus groups was started by some Harvard graduates, and they were aware of studies there on mentoring, and so connected Harvard and Kathleen.

They found a symbiotic relationship; Kathleen wanted information on what was proven and documented to work in mentoring, and the Harvard group wanted an organization to be a willing place for them to study mentoring. This was a part of Harvard's Project IF (Inventing the Future) directed by Dr. Micahael Nakkula. Part of their Risk and Prevention Program to understand how support systems can best help children.

"They were doing a small mentoring program but because they were doing it from an academic stand point they were making some mistakes like enabling people to become dependent on them and we know that you can't do that."

"When you do mentoring it is the volunteer that is the person making the change in the child's life and your job is to support that, and to support the family to go out and get services in the community. You don't want to be the social service person, you don't want to be their psychologist, you don't want to be their social worker. You want to be a conduit to help them access services in the community. You tell them the best thing they can do is go to church, go get involved in a church, any church or synagogue or mosque, or something where you have a community for your children. You can tell them about things like going to the Open Door organization to get some clothes, but not to be the person who is solving their problems."

"That was one of the things they had to learn because they would get overly enmeshed. They were just doing a tiny mentoring program and so weren't getting much of the practical side of what mentoring is. But as far as how do you develop tools that generate valuable research data and at the same time are of value to the Match Adviser, they were way ahead on that piece."

John Harris of ARC Research Consulting was the primary researcher for Harvard doing most of the work with BBBS. Since then Kathleen has occasionally been able to consult other mentoring agencies working with ARC.

They worked with Harvard for several years and a great deal was learned, and that was applied to how YBBBS operates. "We did all that with them years ago and incorporated it. Some of the work we did has become institutionalized. We have a computerized system that tracks a lot of that for you." The National BBBS, in the last couple of years, provides a computerized system for case management that some agencies around the country use that incorporates some of this. "But people don't realize there are holes in that process that if you don't keep them plugged you get false data."

One of the results of that in-depth study is that YBBBS is one of the few social service organizations that have meaningful, documented statistics on the effectiveness of their work. One of Kathleen's pet peeves, from her social science background, is the number of social service efforts—helping organizations, drug abuse prevention programs, and other organizations and programs—that garner a lot of financial support and consume a lot of time, but have no documentation as to whether they are effective.

BBBS has been able to document remarkable effectiveness. The kids in their programs are: 46% Less likely to start using drugs, 27% less likely to start drinking, 52% less likely to skip a day of school, and 60% less likely to get arrested. A local study with BBBS and Juvenile Probation found that kids who are matched to Bigs are half as likely to be arrested. That's comparing an at-risk population of kids, the ones who have one parent or a parent in prison or were referred after getting into legal trouble, with the general population. So that they are half as likely to be arrested is an even bigger success than it first appears.

The agency has grown to now server about 1000 kids, and employes over thirty people.

Brad

It is difficult to get Brad to say exactly how he went about getting YEI going well, after those rough starts. As mentioned, he is more of a doer than a thinker. He just comes across each challenge as it comes up and deals with it. By this point though, he has training in his field, and years of working part-time with mentally challenged kids. With this mental groundwork laid, when he makes those quick decisions they are likely to be sound decisions.

An example of this was a day when there was no contract work going on. What to do with these people? He certainly was not going to send them home. He did not want them just sitting around. Just sitting around is counter-therapeutic for his people, nor something Brad is inclined to do himself. It came to him that there is always volunteer work to be done. He knew that the grounds of a local retirement home needed some picking up. So Brad loaded a bunch of his people into a van, drove up there, announced to the retirement-home staff what they were doing, and set to work.

For most people, the thought to go do volunteer work might have occurred at that point, but not led to immediate action. Perhaps they would make some calls to prepare for some future date. Perhaps make a plan and a schedule and such. Brad just saw a need, a solution, and within the hour the problem was solved and productive work was being done.

Significantly this was not only a solution for the problem of the day but the beginning of an important policy of YEI, as we shall see.

Brad is also an extremely high energy, extroverted, gregarious guy who can talk your ear off and entertain you while he's doing it. He has such an excess of this energy that he plays guitar and sings at local bars and restaurants at least once a week and has developed a good reputation for it. Some people in Prescott who are more attuned to night life only know Brad as a local musician and are surprised to hear he has something to do with social services. This ability to be engaging serves him well in being an endless evangelist for his work. He manages to know a great many people, including many of the right people to be of help to YEI. When he is around them they can not help but be fully aware of his presence and are reminded of his work.

His being outgoing helped make a connection to someone who would be important to YEI, Russ Rusing. Russ was the father of two students at Brophy High School who Brad knew, Tom and Dan Rusing. Brad had met their father, Russ, briefly. Russ ran a very popular bakery and meeting spot, Julie Ann's Bakery. One day Brad heard that Russ was retiring, and he knew Russ was to much of a worker to really retire. So the same day he called up Russ and asked if he could meet him the next day, "to get your opinion on something." He wanted to get Russ together with himself and a couple of key people from YEI and see if Russ would be interested in helping the organization.

He didn't know that Russ already had a favorable impression of YEI. One bad winter day sometime past when Russ was working at his bakery, an employee called to say he couldn't make it in. While the employee is telling him this Russ sees a couple of Brad's guys walking off to work with their lunch buckets. He figured these guys knew how to work.

Russ became a key person in fund raising and the forming of a companion organization, Prescott Charities, and helping YEI to meet the goal of owning their own buildings so they didn't have to pay mortgages.

From a business standpoint YEI has been running a pretty good contract-work business for most of these years. One venture they've had going for several years is building picnic tables and benches. They place them outside numerous businesses around town with a sign that they can be purchased through YEI.

Another business venture they tried was making adobe bricks. It was a successful venture for a while and was highly praised and promoted as a business that could be good for many similar settings; such as work that other rehab centers could do, or that prisoners could do. Not all of that worked out but they did sell bricks for a while and ended up making the bricks to build their own main building.

With a mountain of bricks ready Brad and some friends largely built the main building themselves in a very short time. Those friends were primarily Mr. Dahlberg, who had the camp on Mingus Mountain, and Marshall who is the special ed. director for the school district. These old friendships have proved long lived and productive.

From a service standpoint those first three goals are a small part of what YEI has accomplished. What YEI provides to its customers is a remarkably normal and happy life. That is the guiding principle, "normalcy", that Brad picked up from professor Wolfensbuger and which he has stuck with. To make life as normal as possible for his workers.

When someone comes to YEI they quickly find that they are not a patient or a ward, they are an employee. They work, draw a wage, and pay taxes. They all have titles, with "assembly technician" being the most common. They are all asked to bring a lunch box just like normal people going off to a job. Most of them deal with their lunch just fine. Some need help getting their lunch out of the box and set up or other kinds of help, but in every way they can, as far as they can, they are expected to be normal employees doing normal work things. Walk into one of the workrooms and you find a crew of people around tables assembling widgets and sorting bulk mail in a very orderly and productive way. There are a lot of smiles and friendly chit-chat around those tables.

In addition to efforts for normalcy for the workers while at YEI, a good bit of the off hours time is also spent in normal pursuits. Brad encourages a lot of the activities that would be done by normal people who like working together. So there are sports and dances and other get-togethers. In this spirit of normalization the staff, who would be called counselors, are called job placement assistants, because that's primarily what they do; help these people find jobs, inside YEI or outside.

Another part of the normalness is that a number of the extra hands, who drive the trucks or do other work at YEI, were not hired for their social service experience but just because Brad thought they would be good for the position. Brad has approached people and suggested they come to work for YEI. A typical response is that they don't know anything about working with "those people". Brad's response is that it's no different than working anyplace else. You may have to talk a little slower, you may have to ask them to repeat something you couldn't understand, but other than that it is just a normal job.

That day when Brad took his workers to do volunteer cleanup at the retirement home served as a good precedent for another type of normalization. Brad thinks work is a wonderful therapy and part of a normal life, and that all work has dignity. He quotes Kahlil Gibran that "work is love made visible" or refers to the encyclical of Pope John Paul II on the nature of work. So this apparently off-the-cuff decision to take the crew to do volunteer work was actually grounded in his attitude about work and about normalization. That day turned into an important part of the YEI routine, that all the workers spend some part of every week in volunteer work.

As the this routine continued they discovered it was an even better fit than they had realized. Sitting with the folks at the retirement home works well. If one of the Alzheimer's patients wants to keep telling the same story over and over, Brad's people don't mind. They are excellent listeners. On the other hand, if a patient does not talk much, most of Brad's people, once they get started, are excited to talk at length about their work, or what's going on at home, or anything else that comes to mind. Those residents who like to listen, enjoy hearing about all this.

There is another nice side effect for the workers. His workers need say "thank you" often in the course of the average day. All day long, everyday, they are saying "thank you for driving me to work", "thank you for opening the door for my wheelchair", "thank you for helping me with my lunch". But when they finish cleaning up the grounds somewhere, or disinfecting surfaces at the Pioneer Home rest home, or spending an hour with somebody there, the tables are turned and they hear "thank you" said to them. That lets them know that they are doing things of genuine value.

People who have their own lives working fairly well often give something to others. As Brad points out it is in keeping with psychologist Abraham Maslow's hierarchy of needs. First you need air, then you need food, at a higher level you need inclusion in a group, and at a higher level there is a need to give back. It parallels the scriptural idea "unto whomsoever much is given, of him shall be much required." When these people help others it re-enforces the theme of living a normal, and useful, life.

Brad will say that they sort of stumbled into this idea of volunteer work and then "backed into" the idea that it was great for his people. That is partly true, but had it not been for his training, experience, and what is obviously a good deal of thought about these issues, he might never have "stumbled" on the idea of volunteer work.

This volunteering outside of YEI and striving for normalcy also applies to the jobs they do. In addition to working in the shops at YEI a good few of them have jobs outside, for which YEI acts as an employment agency. To place people in jobs that they will like they try to find out what they would like to do. They will often want to do things that are beyond them, but YEI will connect them with jobs that fill that desire. If they want to be a nurse, YEI may get them a job in the hospital cafeteria. They have a job, a title, a pay check, get to wear the uniform gown, take their lunch box and go to work each day, and life is normal. One fellow wanted to be a policeman. They got him a job in the police station doing simple cleanup. It wasn't easy. These days you have to get clearance from Homeland Security to work in a police station. Plus the job-coach had to be on site especially during training, and she was from Canada. So clearances weren't easy to get.

Another worker wanted to drive heavy equipment. Brad talked to Mike Fann, owner of a local contracting company, and got him a job washing the trucks and equipment. He is really proud of his job. When visiting dignitaries were looking over Brad's successful operation once, he took them out to show how well this guy did washing trucks. One of the visitors noted that there were a lot of trucks lined up and commented to the worker, "that's a lot of trucks to wash." The worker looked at the trucks lined up, thought a minute, and responded, "That's a s... load of trucks." Brad emphasizes to the guys that there are many situations where certain language is inappropriate. Here they were in the truck yard of a construction company with all men, and this worker decided this was not an inappropriate time. He was right.

It has gotten to be a common site around town, one of the Downs Syndrome or other developmentally challenged people walking to or from work with their lunch box in their hand. Or they are cleaning up the trays at a local diner, or out on the corner with a sign for a local business waving and inviting people in. It has also become a common assumption, usually true, that this is another one of "Brad's guys."

Part of what enabled YEI to thrive is a great deal of community support which, as mentioned, Brad does a lot of drumming up. To be fair he says YEI is an easy sell. Mostly he has gotten donations for specific projects, such as building their buildings. When he tries to get such donations he points out that either the community finds constructive ways to give these people productive lives in which they earn a pay check and pay their taxes, or they sit home collecting disability insurance and watching Jerry Springer. People usually see the logic of that and contribute.

Another part of the support is financial mentoring. Brad had no business training. He credits some successful local business people with helping him develop some savvy in that area.

There have been some ups and downs over the years. From time to time Brad will see that some income stream is winding down, as when the adobe brick business reached the end of its usefulness. Or he'll see that some important donors are no longer going to be available or the economy is generally going down and donations are going to be harder to get. It may be that some key person in the organization is feeling the need to move on, though this is rare. Plus there is always competition for the assembly work his people do with cheaper services overseas.

One of his long time customers came to him some years back and said that competitors were having their assembly done overseas at significant savings and under-selling him. He was practically in tears when he told Brad that for his business to survive he had to send his assembly overseas too.

Generally when these downturns are on the horizon he has been able to attend to those problems in advance and not let things go to far. There have been lean times though. Brad knows what it is like to have to lay people off. For the sake of the organization, at those times, the lay offs were not based on seniority, but on who was most essential.

Just a few years back, though, was one of those downturns that was especially bad in some ways. Several things happened at once. There were some tight times on the horizon for the organization, Brad's marriage ended, and he got deathly ill.

It got to the point that, in a hospital room in Phoenix, Brad tried to fill in his staff as best he could about how to run the things he tended to, in case he didn't come back. He was completely out of commission as far as YEI was concerned for the better part of three months. He told his staff that the running of things was not that hard and there wasn't that much knowledge to pass on. In a superficial way that may have been true. But then there's a lot of hard experience that had gone into doing those things right. But from another angle things were not that bad. Most of Brad's staff had a long history with the organization and lot of experience of their own.

When he first returned to work he found them painting the interior. He was pleasantly surprised. Often when an organization is leaderless for a while things start to slip. Far from slipping, they were improving things. Brad got back into the swing of things and between he and his staff they made a nice recovery.

The service YEI provides to the community is better than the rehab service available in many larger communities. In some communities they keep developmentally challenged students in special ed. classes until they are 22. Brad finds that ridiculous. They have a challenge fitting in to begin with. As they get to be considerably older than their classmates in the same grade they are physically much bigger and it makes it even more awkward to fit in.

In addition, while learning as much as they can is a good thing, Brad finds the endless classes in pretending to teach them something that is beyond them makes no sense. They ought to get on with the lives they are going to have. They are sometimes kept in endless reading classes when they have no chance of learning to read. Brad's philosophy is to be realistic. For instance he likes to play guitar. He figures God hasn't given him enough talent to play for the Rolling Stones, but enough to perform at Coyote Joe's, a local bar, on a regular basis. Same thing with these kids. God says they're not going to learn to read, but they can work and live remarkably normal lives. So why not get on with it.

To give one example of how YEI operates, a woman moved into the area with a special needs adult-child. Her realtor told her about YEI. Immediately after pulling the U-Haul truck into the driveway of her new home she called from her cell phone to get information or get on a waiting list. Brad talked to her and explained they had one of their work vans going out to get some people and it could swing by and pick up her son. She could focus on getting moved in and he could come check out YEI.

The van picked him up and brought him to YEI where they explained he would be an employee with a paycheck and a title, and he started working. He was very proud when he got home and explained to his mother he was an "employee". She was ecstatic. They city she had moved from had had her son on waiting lists for nine years. And that was just to get into some day care type of facility where they would have been doing nothing that would have given her son a sense of worth.

In many facilities in other cities patients may spend day after day on craft projects that are of no real worth to anyone. Or they are in endless classes teaching things these people are not up to learning. Or they have what Brad says the industry calls "mall therapy". They take a bus load of patients to the mall to go out and socialize. But mostly what they do is sit around the central areas and kill time. People walk by and see a group of them killing time and think, "those poor people". Quite a contrast from the impression of many people in Prescott who see these people going off to work each day with their lunch box in their hand.

Another difference is that many facilities rely primarily on the state's funding of rehab services. For YEI that is just one income stream. They are a business besides. This allows YEI to take the approach of, no waiting, no fees. As with the experience with the mother in the U-Haul, there is no waiting list. YEI starts taking care of them first and then tries to get the state to pick up its share of the tab afterward. In a simple conversation Brad quickly gets an initial feel of whether this is a person who needs, and who fits, their program. He can tell right away if it's someone who needs their program. In some few cases the person is so completely physically disabled that YEI is not a workable place for them. Or in a few cases where behavior is uncontrollable they are too disruptive to the rest of the workers. Even then though they will try to make it work, try to bring in an extra assistant who pretty much just babysits that one person and tries to get them on track to fitting into YEI.

As baby boomers retire it is becoming common for people with adult special needs children to be looking into various communities to retire too, and one of the criteria they look at is whether there are good facilities for their child. Prescott has that covered in YEI. New people looking for services show up about two times a month typically, and anyone who fits the program is immediately accepted. There are no fees to the parents.

Beyond just taking them into the program the staff at YEI try to see that whatever their workers need is taken care of. If one of the workers who is living in the men's house or doesn't have parents around anymore, or has parents on limited income, has dental problems they'll try to attend to it. They will try getting state health care to cover it, or if not they will see if some local dentist will donate the work, or if they have tapped out that resource then YEI will pay for it directly and figure out the finances later. As Brad says, "It's nice not having to say 'no' to whatever his guys need, if things are sufficiently funded."

Over the years he and his staff have well exceeded Brad's original goals. YEI served about 14 people when he arrived. It now serves about 140. For some types of services that would not be a large number. A health clinic for instance only sees most patients for a short time until they're better, or long term patients only occasionally, so the total number of patients considered active might be large. But in the case of a rehab center, these are 140 people who spend all day, every day, working with Brad and his staff, plus all the outside time they spend together. For these 140 their whole lives are improved by being in YEI.

The goals of owning their own building and being financially stable have been achieved in spades too. They recently had their six buildings appraised at $5.5 million dollars. They owe no mortgage payments.

Besides not owning mortgage they also own their vans and vehicles outright. They have a shop in neighboring Prescott Valley on 5 acres with 6600 square feet of building space. They have a 5000 square foot group home for a half dozen of the guys right up the street from their main building. A wonderful couple manages the home. They have a similar home for some of the gals named "Rusing Hills" after Russ Rusing.

The program at the Prescott Valley location is going well but Brad hopes to remodel that building soon to make things work even better there. He finds that it's very important to have a pleasant working environment for his people. The arrangement in Prescott Valley works, but not as well as he'd like. Not as well as it works in the main Prescott building. For the people he's helping it's all about creating a place where being happy and productive comes naturally. The environment they are in plays an important role, perhaps especially so with these people.

They also have some space near the Prescott air park, which is in a location triangulated between Prescott, Prescott Valley, and Chino Valley. It's where much big industrial growth is likely to happen. Brad likes to be near where the business is. The location in Prescott Valley is right near Better Built Aluminum which is one of the larger industrial businesses there, and YEI provides a great deal of service to them.

LATER YEARS AND
AFTER THOUGHTS

John

Toward the end of his time there CSS had about 120 staff in offices all over Northern Arizona. One of the last projects was to get accreditation with an organization for family and juvenile services, similar to the kind of accreditation a hospital has to maintain. In order to reach that they had to meet over 1,100 standards. When their on-site review came up they did the best of any agency in the country.

There is also some sense of disappointment. "Toward the end of my time there it began to be different. I'd say, 'let's all go over and paint the shelter' and some would say, 'we're not going to paint the shelter. Hire someone.' But we could save some money doing it ourselves."

Thinking about the others in this group, of Kathleen he says, "I always thought she had one of the best documented, successful programs and was real helpful to kids. I see Brad sometimes at family functions since he and my wife are cousins. I see Gordon at church a lot. I did some services for him early on, services for kids in the juvenile system."

On what prepared him for this career, "I went to a very good high school that prepared me for a lot of things, both intellectually and spiritually. It was a tough place to get through. Academically very difficult. They weren't kidding when they said you had to study threes hours a night to get through. From talking to kids it's still true."

"There's a great book called Heroic Leadership written by an ex-Jesuit priest. There are four main tenants in it, which are things that have always been part of my life. I've always wondered if the Jesuits gave those to us and we didn't know it, if they just slipped them in. One is to do a self assessment everyday, how did you do, what did you do. I don't do it every day but I do consider how can I do more, where am I weak, how can I strengthen that."

"The second is having a world view, and acceptance of people and their differences. The third thing was to always have a heroic goal. It doesn't have to be a 'save the world' kind of goal. It can be small and personal, but kind of impossible. The last tenant is a basic love of mankind. I find if I can bring keep that idea, bring it into a given situation, that works real well for me all the time."

"I may sound like a real religious guy, but I'm not. I do some things. I pray a lot. The Jesuits teach you to pray on the fly. They don't want you wasting your time sitting around not doing anything. I can be driving down the street praying as I go, and some guy will cut me off and I'll start yelling at him. In that sense I'm not a real religious guy."

"Ignatius Loyola wrote the Jesuits' manual. It was 240 pages long, for an order that at that time was 15 people. 180 of those pages are about how to select the right person." That kind of fit his style. He didn't considered himself competent in all areas so, "I would want to get someone in who really knew what they were doing for whatever the need was."

One thing he was good at was budgeting. He would teach budgeting to the other directors. But for other needs he would search for someone who was smart, intelligent, hard working, and persistent. If they had those things they could probably learn whatever else they need for their job. "I had probably heard that that was Loyola's approach but didn't really think about it until reading it later."

Once he had the right people hired, "Then my job was to not screw those people up, to stay out of their way, to help them. If someone was starting out in this field that's what I would tell them. It's who you pick. If you want a good counselor find someone who has some values and drives to them, and kind of a caring and love for people. It's hard to interview for those kind of things. Those are gut judgments. The worst hire we ever did was on one of these formula systems based on points for different things. The initial, fundamental foundation you build everything on is who you hire."

"Loyola would send people to China to teach whatever they needed, as a way to get in. Then maybe people would be curious about what else they had to offer. So it takes people who can dive in and not be afraid. I think I've always had that."

"You have to grow too. You don't start out with the same emotional quality and intellectual quality and value quality at twenty two that you hopefully have at fifty or fifty-five or whatever. You grow over time and that richness is important. There's a lot of things you need to do on your own, to struggle through and learn on your own, but if you have that innate intelligence then you can do that, you'll get through that kind of stuff."

One other ingredient John says a person needs starting out in a career like his is a firm commitment to be in a helping profession and the drive to stick with it and overcome the challenges along the way. "I'd also tell somebody starting out you'd better have that drive or it's going to kill you. If you really don't want it, it's going to kill you, or you won't do it."

Catholic Social Services is now called Catholic Charities, as it had been in the past, and John likes that name.

Max

As Max looks back on his work he touches on an assortment of milestones, changes, and factors in his career.

"While I was supervisor we handled 13,000 or 14,000 cases of abuse or neglect. Maybe 3000 were sexual abuse, another 3000 physical abuse, and the rest neglect. So about half neglect. Some cases were of kids who died, and they stick with you. I try to forget the cases but a couple of them were really sad and I still remember them."

"The social problems changed over the years. When I first started the main issue was drinking. Now it's crystal meth."

"When an allegation came in we had a priority system. We would evaluate it and set its priority which would determine how fast we would respond. The highest priority calls had to be responded to within two hours, but actually we would respond to those faster, as fast as we could. These cases we also reported to the police department."

"Originally when someone wanted to report a possible case of abuse or neglect they just called me up and we evaluated it. During the 90s that changed to a centralized intake, which was hard for us to accept, and hard for the community to accept. To report a possible problem it had to be called down to central intake in Phoenix. That was done partly for economy, and partly so there would be a standardized way of doing intake."

"But I liked doing our own evaluation. For one thing urban standards were a little different. They filtered out more possible cases, I think partly because they didn't have the man-power. Here we would respond to more calls and would try to look into it and see if there really was a problem. Also some calls didn't have enough information for us to respond to. Maybe some teacher just had a feeling there was a problem. In a case like that I could work with the teacher to see if some additional evidence was available to make a substantial enough cause for us to respond to it. So that personal communication was good. On the other hand we used to have to keep someone in the office to answer any calls that came in. When they started central intake, that freed up that worker to be out in the field."

"One change that happened more after I left was under Governor Napolitano more emphasis was put on safety of the children, less inclination to leave the child with the family if there was doubt. That was partly an adaption to seeing more drug problems and the decision to be quicker about removing kids from those families."

"My interest in social service was influenced by my time working with kids who worked at Tuzigoot Monument when I worked there as a student, but I was already considering that kind of work out of influence from the 60s, of wanting to make a difference."

"My childhood also was part of that. I was always very close to my parents, and I had a really good childhood."

"I did try to avoid the draft. College helped with that. I wouldn't have gone to Canada if I'd been called up, but it would have crossed my mind had I been drafted. I didn't participate in demonstrations, but I had a lot of questions about why we were in Vietnam. We had that lottery system and I had a very high number so I felt good about that."

Some people he remembers: "Rob Ameln who, with his wife Mary, was one of the Vista volunteers who started Big Brothers, after that Vista contract was up, came to work for CPS for a couple of years. He later moved South and was in charge of CPS for Pima County and stayed with that until he retired."

"The lady who hired me was Verna Watson. She was in her seventies at the time, and had been involved in Yavapai County welfare services since the 1930s."

"Ken and Evelyn Smith from Chino Valley were great foster parents. They were at it for a long time and did a good job of it. They've adopted lots of kids and had hundreds of foster kids."

There connection with social service is not over either: "Lindsay works at the Guidance Clinic. Not in direct social service but in administration. One of my daughters works there and is a case worker."

"I recently bumped into someone at the county transfer station who remembered me as being involved in her adoption some twenty or thirty years ago. I asked her how she had done. She said she had a pretty good childhood."

Don

The growth of paperwork over the years vexed Don. "I had been battling paperwork for ten of my twenty nine years. I had kind of a lesson learned. Through my activities at the state level, we have a trade group and have a dialog with the state entities and do training and such, and I was active in that. Using that angle I got some of my counterparts around the state together and we said we had to do something about the paperwork. It's costing us, it's meaningless, it's offensive, it's crazy. So I get three or four other CEOs together and we get our organizations to put leverage on the state on that issue. We said to them, 'Please, this is out of control.' Every time you turn around it's one more piece of paper, and one more demand, and ultimately it takes away from service. I had pounded away at this for four or five years. Finally the Department of Health Services set up a committee to address this problem. If you've heard such stories before, you're going to hear it one more time. What happened was the committee decided to add paper."

How you have to be good at more than just social services. "One of my buddies whom I really respect runs the programs in Navajo County, and he and I have traveled all over the country together professionally. He describes the reality of the work in mental health care in Arizona as operating in a socio/eco/political environment. It's something we should be more aware of in the day-to-day operations with our staff and our boards. You would think the job is to identify a need and satisfy the need through the best services you can apply. That seems pretty simple, but that's not the way it is at all. It's a political environment. You can never do it that cleanly. You've always got this burden of the system shaping that service in some way, or precluding it, or limiting it in some way that's largely political."

About the need to connect with elected officials and how Don's skill at it grew. "You live in Okawville or Addieville and you march to what other people tell you to do and you don't have a lot of influence on your future, and you sure as heck don't approach a political leader and ask for something. You might complain a lot to each other, but not to them. So I bring all that baggage along and here I am, being told over and over that our money comes from the state, you'd better pay attention. And I didn't know how to do that. So I had learn how to do that, just trial by fire."

"But it's true in Arizona, maybe everywhere, but it was in Arizona when I had to learn those skills, it was a pretty friendly place. Legislators were accessible and John Hays, Lucy Mason, Ken Bennett, Carol Springer and others saw a part of their role was to have those connections. So I made it out to be a lot harder than it was. It was all about a relationship and just and being respectful to people. And expecting them to be respectful to you. And by and large they have been."

"You choose your battles and you're always respectful, but you go in with the idea that they need the information you have. As long as you're providing straight and accurate information they're going to benefit from what you're telling them. As often as not they'll call you and say, for instance, 'I'm hearing about all this meth use up in Prescott. Is it really as bad as people say it is or not?' It wasn't that hard of a lesson but it seemed really daunting to me at the time, really unfamiliar territory. But guys like John Hays made it easy because of their openness and the respect they would show you. That's been true of Ken Bennett and Lucy Mason and all of them going back before."

On staying positive: "An axiom I adopted early on goes something like this: 'First the hopeless client attempts to render the counselor hopeless; so that both can then, and forevermore, wallow in a state of hopelessness.' I think human services professionals often fall into that trap. It is, after all, easier to cave in to hopeless circumstances than to remain positive and hopeful. My peers refused to operate from that hopeless perspective. In the end, it made our jobs easier and more effective when we reached out to the others for solutions. Columbine is a good example. We could say it could happen here but there's nothing we can do about it because it's hopeless. You just can't let that happen."

On staying connected to the patients: "One of my approaches to the work, that I sometimes think was a detriment at times, was my need to in some way connect with the patients in a pretty direct way. When I started and the clinic was small I saw patients and carried a case load and did crisis work and all. Even when we had 260 some employees, a $20 million budget, I still could not help myself but engage with those patients in some way. I couldn't do it very much but I always did it."

"The reason I say it could be a detriment is partly because it takes time away from managing, but also because it can kind of screw things up because you're entering the system several rungs down and all. I managed to do it to a small extent by stepping into service delivery in a very direct way. It might come about because some patient is unhappy or a particularly complicated case. It would be natural for me to get involved at the administrative level to see if everything has been done. But at some point I'd say I just can't deal with the abstract, I'm going to go and meet that patient. I'd just go and visit them."

"It's an almost irreconcilable dilemma. The company is large. The demands are great. You've got to maintain your objectivity because you're dealing with numbers of people, and you can't possibly have relationships with all those people like you could in a small company or in a small family. So you are compelled to distance yourself in some manner from the trenches. By time, by job description, by competing demands. But on the other hand the end product of your company, whether you're marketing, selling, getting paid to do, is all about these end users. And about to what extent your company is connecting with them in some meaningful way. So how do you stay in touch with your customer in some meaningful way? It was just part of my experience which was kind of a push and pull. I would love to have had a case load twenty nine years later, but that wasn't in the cards."

"That same focus on direct connection led to another idea. Sheila Polk, the Yavapai County Attorney, said she didn't know much about how addiction is actually treated and could I explain it to her. I said, let's get some of the meth users who are in the treatment programs together and we'll ask them, what's this illness all about? What's your experience? What got you into this mess? And what's your experience of the treatment?"

"We thought it would be a great idea but we ran into the problem that many of these people were being prosecuted through her office. So we did the next best thing and got four staff members who have achieve recovery and got them together. We all got together in a room and ask them about their experience. It was a powerful lesson. And it has shaped this whole MATForce program. When we entered the room to have this talk, Sheila and my staff person, Kathy Tootle immediately recognized each other from when Sheila was a staff prosecutor and handled Kathy's case. Kathy Tootle makes no secret of this. She was a willing part of a front page article about the problem. It was very touching because what Kathy Tootle was able to say to Sheila, and the rest of us who were privileged to be there, was that, 'you always treated me with respect'. She also talked about the respect that judge Kuebler showed her."

On how the group worked together: "Looking back, I think we were all a bunch of young professionals who each had enormous responsibilities, but not a lot of experience. And, being new grads, we were trained to operate in our little corner of the Human Services world. We were probably pretty idealist and thought we had the silver bullets to make things right for those in need. And then reality sets in. You learn that people are complex and people problems are exponentially complex. You begin to realize that troubled kids need stable relationships as well as counseling; you figure out that people with mental illness need housing and jobs as well as treatment; you know that juvenile offenders need counseling, flexible educational services and positive role models. You learn that parents who neglect their kids often have substance abuse treatment needs and that neglected children need counseling and advocates...and so it goes. If you try to operate on an island, you're going to be unsuccessful in addressing these complex needs. As we matured, I think we used each other to expand our reach and stretch the resources."

And finally, on leadership and passion: "I think there's an art, or a less definable leadership quality which is that, 'I personify the mission. I believe in what I'm doing so deeply that you can't dismiss me as just a bean counter that doesn't care'. Kathy and Brad certainly have that. And I think the way you do that, is you probably can't help yourself. That's part of what I'm saying too about my experience is you can't help yourself, you just have to do it. And you do it because it's the way you nurture that passion, so you hang in there in times of trouble."

Gordon

Gordon, too, spoke highly of the judges he worked with over the time. "I worked with six different presiding juvenile court judges over the years. Each one had his own philosophy, but all were geared toward helping juveniles succeed, while protecting the community at the same time. It was my job as middle-management to follow the judge's philosophy. Something that helped me over the years, was to meet with each new judge as they came in and provide a good orientation of our operation. I also assured each judge that he was the chief administrator of the juvenile court and we would follow his philosophical direction."

"All of our judges liked the direction we were going, but they weren't necessarily satisfied with the status quo either. They wanted things to progress, to try new things and to learn from them. That was refreshing because that always interested me. I was never one to just sit still and put something out there and just sit on it. I always wanted to try new things and develop new programs. The judges were very supportive of that."

"I was blessed, really, with working for six outstanding juvenile court judges: Judge Paul Rosenblatt, Judge James Hancock, Judge James Sult, Judge Ray Weaver, Judge Richard Anderson, and Judge Robert Brutinel. The judges couldn't have been better. They always had the best interest of the juveniles at heart."

Clearly, the developing and improving of programs to improve the chances of good outcomes of the juveniles in his charge was a priority, and a source of pride. "We had many good programs over the years. We were constantly evaluating. I think that was very important. We probably didn't do as good of a job as we should have, but we always were reviewing our programs and offerings and trying to improve upon them If they weren't working, we would scrap them. If they were, we would build upon their successful components."

"There were both internal and external reviews and evaluations of our programs and operation. The internal reviews were conducted on an on-going basis by our staff while the external reviews/evaluations were conducted by an outside agency. There was a big external review of juvenile justice statewide in the 90s which was commissioned by the legislature. We came out smelling like a rose."

"We would also send out quality satisfaction surveys to parents of our kids and to the kids themselves. We got their feedback on the services they received as well as their satisfaction with the probation officer."

Gordon talked about the others in this group of six: "Juvenile Probation used the Guidance Clinic a lot, even before Don O. was there. We were always real close to WYGC because they would take our clients for free. When we started acquiring some funding to pay for services, we did so. But we always had an understanding, especially with Don, that our funding was limited and that our families would continue to receive services even when our funds were exhausted. Don developed a sliding scale for families to receive services based on their ability to pay, which allowed us to serve even more families."

"So we developed a lot of programs with WYGC over the years. Specialized programs, a first-offender program called Juvenile Education Project where a first-offender would come in for a six hour program at the Guidance Clinic that was educational in nature. The beauty of that program was that at least one parent had to accompany the juvenile. They would go over the offense in a group setting, going over what got them into this situation and what they needed to do to stay out of it in the future. WYGC also offered intensive outpatient programs for substance abuse. A lot of our issues with kids are related to substance abuse. The West Yavapai Guidance Clinics were very instrumental in helping us develop those programs. We wouldn't be nearly as effective as we are without them, including the Verde Valley Guidance Clinic, as well."

"One of our earlier programs was the Volunteers in Probation Program through Yavapai Big Brothers/Big Sisters. We initially ran the program ourselves which was modeled after one in Colorado called 'Partners'. We saw the benefit, in the 70s, of having a mentor, an adult figure who could replace a lost parent, or a parent who couldn't step up to be that role model for these kids. So we started doing it and it was very time consuming to match kids with a Big Brother or Big Sister one-on-one. Then it finally dawned on us that BBBS is going strong. It's tighter in that they have their own screening process. They can be more assured that they're getting a volunteer that's not going to hurt the kids. And so we tied-in with Kathy, in the 70s."

"That program is still going. A very positive program for kids. The downside, like anything else, is they can't get enough volunteers and so kids have to wait a period of time. Some of our kids don't have that luxury of time. They're right on the brink. They're already out there offending and creating problems. They need some help right now. And it takes a certain kind of individual to deal with a kid at that level. With most of the kids BBBS matches they just need someone to go throw a baseball and such. Our kids come with their baggage. We put some things in place, developed monthly activities, probably twice a month that our kids would be engaged in to tide them over till they got a volunteer. So they were put into something with some structure, that they could at least start taking part in something productive until they got their volunteer. It became a high priority with Kathy to get these kids matched as quickly as possible."

"We would pay a certain fee when we referred a kid, so they could do the intake and assessment. But the payment would then stop until the match was made. This provided an added incentive for BBBS to match the juvenile as soon as possible. The program was very effective and productive. Kathy's organization has gotten a number of good evaluations. The program became a pilot for the state in the early 90s. Kathy and I hit the road and went around and talked to all the other probation departments in the state. A number of them joined in and started their own programs modeled after ours. They are still going strong."

"Regarding Child Protective Services with Max, in other areas of the state there's friction sometimes between CPS and us, Juvenile Probation. The reason is because sometimes we're dealing with the same kids. Sometimes there's a different slant or approach on money issues. CPS is largely a social service whereas Juvenile Probation is an arm of the court and is a judicial function. Probably a bit harder; more accountability-driven. So sometimes where there would be friction is if a kid needed a higher level of care, then there were money issues. Maybe there's a kid in foster care who started breaking the law. Now he's coming into our system, and we're trying to get CPS to deal with that kid where he's living. They are saying, 'No, he's yours now. He's breaking the law, so you're responsible.' And he's already got so much baggage that we're looking at a higher cost residential treatment program, a higher level of care. We can't afford that. So there are a lot of tug of war issues over money."

"Max and I were able to bridge the conflicts a lot over the years. I'll say very honestly that Yavapai County was the envy of a lot of counties because Max and I were able to keep the conflicts and friction to a minimum. We didn't sit down and agree to everything but we had a mutual respect for each other's positions. I would say, 'Max, we just don't have the money for that'. He would understand and accept that rather than push the bill. And vice versa. If Max said, 'You know we can't control this kid', we could step up and do what we could. So we would talk to each other on a kid by kid basis and develop a good plan."

"It took a good relationship, especially with Max and me because there was friction between the agencies, and historical friction over the years. Max and I didn't have a lot of friction. We accept each other's position where we were at, and limitations, and went from there. We developed a program, probably the first in the state, where we would split payment on dually-adjudicated youth. Drove the financial people crazy. But for kids involved with both of our agencies and who needed a higher, more costly, level of care, this was a very practical solution."

"When there were differences between the probation officer and the CPS case worker, Max and I would step in and settle that in short order. There's not going to be any this turf battle stuff. Sit down, figure out what the kid and the family needs and what we could offer, and accept that, accept each other's limitations. Over the years there were a handful of times we'd have meetings with all of our staffs, where we would bring our whole departments together and hammer out some issues. The judge had jurisdiction over both kinds of kids, dependents and delinquents so he certainly appreciated it that we could get along."

"With Brad at Yavapai Exceptional Industries we didn't have a lot of direct dealing. Being such an entrepreneur, he developed many wonderful programs for his clientele. He developed his adobe brick business and we would send some kids down to do some community service work occasionally. The kids would hate it because it was hard work. But we didn't have a lot of direct overlap with Brad, nor with John at Catholic Social Services. In later years CSS started to contract with Child Protective Services which increased our collaboration. CSS also assisted us with runaways by funding a bus ticket to get the juvenile home."

"With all these folks (the six) one thing we've shared is a positive relationship, collectively and individually. I think, to be effective, it's all about relationships, to be effective. By that I don't meant the good ol' boy kind of thing at all. I mean the mutual understanding and respect, and the acceptance of limitations; what you can provide, what you can't. And acknowledgment of what we're all trying to do."

"We were somehow able to develop these positive relationships in this era. If there was an issue we could call and they were responsive to that. There was no turf protection and barriers. We could just sit down and get it resolved in short order. Because we're all trying to help families and kids. That was our emphasis. We had an additional task of protecting the community, being a probation department, but they accepted and understood that."

"It's tough to do that but the area, the Yavapai County area, has always been especially conducive to that. It's been easier here, I think, than other places, to forge those relationships. I think they can still do it. It wasn't just limited to this bygone era where this handful of us happened to work in this business for so many years. I still see the guy who took my place, Scott Mabery, still doing the same thing with the Guidance Clinic, with the same folks. Maybe he got that from me and from us, I don't know, but this area is just more conducive to it, I think, than in Phoenix and bigger areas."

"It's that way here probably because of the culture. I think people here are friendly and neighborly. Maybe it was the roots; the people who'd been in the business a long time or lived here a long time. I don't know. People are more real here maybe than in a bigger area, not as invisible. And I think that's still there. It's not just limited to this group of six. Whether it's the sheriff or whoever, they're all able to call one another and just deal with it. There's not a lot of turf protection."

"I don't think you can get away with stuff, being a smaller area, either. If I wanted to just be an ass and not get along with people, I don't think I could have survived. I think you've got to—in order to make your job work in a somewhat effective manner—you've got to develop those relationships."

"The other thing I tried to do internally was to give my people the skills that they needed to carry on our direction, our philosophy, because they're the ones doing it. It was a big decision for me to move from a probation officer to an administrator, because I liked working with kids and families. Loved it. I made a decision that I could still help kids and families indirectly by having good services and people. That's the other piece, not only having resources to send people too, but have your staff who share this mission, and breathe it, and get in there and follow along with it."

"That is partly due to the people we picked. I would much rather have somebody who didn't have a wealth of experience but had the personality that I thought would fit into our mission. You can train them how to be a probation officer and give them all the fundamental knowledge and information about their tasks, but they've got to have the ability to believe in our mission and to really live that direction. We'd hit them hard on that."

"The other part is we'd spend a lot of time involving people in direction and decision making. It wasn't an autocratic environment where I would say this is the way it's going to be, take it or leave it. Get on the ship or get off and hit the road. We spent a tremendous amount of time in buy-ins, in setting that direction. I had a vision of what I wanted to do, but was very much oriented toward making the department part of that decision making process. It wouldn't always go down the direction I thought it would go, might go some other way. But that was a key part in the thing was giving them some say in the direction we were going. That takes a lot of time, a lot of meetings, a lot of committee work, a lot of bullshit, but you need to do that in order to get that buy-in."

"Mostly it went along the path we went because we had the people who shared the vision and it's just a matter of continuing along that and giving them a say in it. But the bigger you get the harder it becomes because then you have different groups. Detention officers, probation officers, support staff, program staff, and trying to get the department wide buy-in becomes tough. It costs a lot of money to have a meeting and bring in all the staff, and we were conscious of tax-payer money. But it was important to be effective to have everybody along the same path, have a say in it. That was big for me."

About innovation: "We did both some innovation on our own and some looking at successful programs in other places. There were blue ribbon programs evaluated and put out nationally by the office of Juvenile Justice out of the federal Department of Justice that were showcased. We had an opportunity to look at some of those. Of course we always modified them to our local needs and community because everywhere is different and unique. There was also the ability to look at programs statewide. We had a strong network statewide of probation directors, still going on, where we would meet about programs and operational stuff. It's a good network to share information of what's working and what's not in different areas."

"The Administrative Office of the Supreme Court, became very instrumental in securing funding for the probation department statewide along with some federal funding. Also in assisting with evaluation and showcasing programs that were working within the state as well as outside the state. But yeah, we would steal ideas and concepts and programs, we certainly would, as well as innovating on our own."

"One thing as far as local innovations, there was the Juvenile Accountability Act in the 90s, with a big emphasis on getting tougher on juvenile crime, holding kids more accountable, and transferring them to adult court quicker for certain offenses. Part of the emphasis was federal, so the federal government would send some money to the state for the states to enact some laws to do that. Arizona was one of first to do that. So we had a pretty sizable pocket of money coming into the state. Our approach was to seek input from not only our staff, but from the stake holders, the judge, the county attorney, the defense attorneys, the school folks, the police departments, and say, 'Where are the gaps? This is what we've got. This money is coming in. What can we really benefit from?'"

"We had a number of meetings and came up with consensus to start a Juvenile Accountability Crew. It was similar as our community service work crews in that we would supervise a group of juveniles throughout the day. However, instead of doing community service, the Juvenile Accountability Crew was program-packed. We utilized a number of paid service providers and volunteers to offer programming in a number of different areas to the juvenile participants."

"We also started a Community Advisory Board which was a group of citizens, including youth, who had in interest in young people and juvenile justice. This group became our advisers and our advocates. They were very helpful in developing programs, reviewing our operation and educating the public about juvenile justice and the issues facing young people. Our Community Advisory Board is one of my proudest accomplishments."

"Some of our ideas spread to other counties, like the Volunteers In Probation Program with BBBS and our employment program. We also got calls from many counties requesting our policy and procedure manual and our training and orientation modules for their replication."

"We've grown from a fairly basic operation with just those few people at the start, to a pretty sophisticated program with a lot of stakeholders and people and resources and money. When I left I think there were twenty seven probation officers, and sixty nine total people in the department. As I mentioned, the Administrative Office of the Supreme Court is the administrative body of the court statewide and a lot of the funding flows through them to us. So we have influences of control that come into play."

"My view is that they are there to support us. They are the administrative body. I was always big on maintaining local autonomy, letting us develop what works for Yavapai County. However, local autonomy sometimes conflicts with statewide uniformity and the Administrative Office of the Courts sometimes required a level of uniformity. So there were some conflicts but overall a spirit of cooperation prevailed."

"You had to step up to the plate to lobby, fight, advocate, whatever to get your share of the money, and then getting your share of the money was only part of it; you wanted it with as few strings as possible so you could do some things with it. Most of our dealings were with the Supreme Court's Administrative Office and by and large they viewed their role the same as I do, it was pretty conducive to cooperation. They could put up a heck of a road block, but most of the people they've had were understanding, and willing to let us do our own thing."

"There were some legislators over the years that took more interest in probation and juvenile justice. Tom Smith, who was in the legislature, was a big advocate and started the Safe Schools program where you put probation officers and police officers in schools to do some law related education and similar things. Not their traditional role of enforcement and security, but rather to work with kids in a different capacity."

"Then you had Governor Fife Symington who, in my view, set our state way back through his movement to get tougher on juvenile crime. He launched the Stop Juvenile Crime Initiative. said we have to get tougher on kids, more kids needed to be transferred to adult court, juvenile justice isn't working,blah, blah, blah. I think that set us way back because studies have shown that juvenile justice in Arizona was, in fact, working and effective. I personally believe he used this Initiative as a platform to get re-elected, which didn't work anyway."

"Fortunately, again in Yavapai County, we had a real good relationship with the County Attorney's office, and they said, 'We still believe in you, in juvenile justice. We're not going to do a wholesale transfer of juveniles to adult court.' We would sometimes transfer. The judge always had the ability to do that. And we'd send a half-dozen to a dozen kids a year to the adult system that we could not contain. They were violent offenders. With this program that discretion went from the judges to the County Attorney. They had the potential of moving hundreds of kids to the adult system if they wanted to, but they said 'no'."

On fitting people and jobs to each other. "Probation Officers, as an example, I always told them that to find happiness here you're going to have to be happy as a probation officer, and there's not a lot of ability to climb any ladder. We were a very flat organization. I would tell them if they were interested in doing a more administrative type of thing you're probably not in the right department. We don't have the ability to do that. That's changed a little bit. We've got more of a ladder now, but I had a real flat organization, just me and my staff. Now they've got more supervisors and an assistant director. That's probably good but that just wasn't my style."

"In any organization there's a tendency to promote by seniority, maybe even the senior position, to take the person that's got the most seniority or been there the longest, to move them into this higher level position. Those don't always match. A probation officer can't always be a good director. That takes different skills. I was lucky I was able to make that transition. But that's a lesson to learn; take a look at the job description of the position you're trying to fill and make sure that person posses those abilities and skill."

"Our promotions were often the most senior people anyway, but maybe that was because we had an array of good people who would have that ability. Scott Mabery, who took my place, was a probation officer then a probation supervisor. He had a lot of the same vision and people skills to excel in that position. I had a real good relationship with him and was very pleased he was selected. It would have been tough for me to walk away after 31 years and have the place go to hell."

"That transition was a lot easier for me because it was somebody that I hired and had trained for ten years. I was a big advocate of doing that. If there's somebody who has the abilities and skills within the department, to go with that person rather than a shinny outsider that you don't know anything about, but looks real good. And the judge agreed with me on that. The judge is the one that made the appointment, Judge Brutinel. There was some good competition, both from within and from without. I was involved in the screening process but I wasn't involved in the interviewing process or the final selection, and I didn't want to. But I did know who the finalists were and I told the judge he was in a great position, having these candidates that look great and he probably couldn't go wrong with any of them. But I had told the judge that if you have someone internally that has the skills and ability to do it, that would be my preference."

"I wanted the place to be set up where it would have a good leader. I accept the fact that I don't have any control over what happens now and if they go on a different path, they go on a different path, but it's nice to think that they'll continue with this philosophy of helping kids and families rather than slamming them. There's a big push statewide to become more law enforcement oriented. It's a very delicate balance between rehabilitation and accountability or punishment. And there's a big push to get tougher and tougher and more supervision and surveillance, and the money starts to go that way rather than to the rehabilitation side. So you have to keep balance to it, and I think Scott has the ability to keep that balance. I hope so. But if it starts to go too much, it does. I don't have any control over it."

Brad

Brad's thought pattern is as active as he is, so pinning him down to a few key statements about what has made it all work is not easy, but across many bits of his telling of how things happened and how they work you can see the spirit of attitude that has guided it all to success.

Early in his time in Prescott he heard people talk about the need to have jobs here to keep the local kids from moving away. That prompted him to say about the kids he was working with, "How do we keep *these* kids in town? So we don't shuffle them off to the state institution?" His solution has been to create jobs for them.

About how some cities use that "mall therapy" described earlier, "It's called 'mall therapy'. And this morning, in Arizona, there are hundreds of people like ours that are in malls, with staff, and they're sitting by the fountain, and they're just sitting there. It's called 'community interaction'. It just sets our movement back because hundreds of people walk by and they go, 'look at those guys. That's them. That's what they do.' But in Prescott, Arizona there's not a week goes by that somebody doesn't say, 'I saw one of your guys walking to work, he's got his lunch box, and he looks like he's got somewhere to go'. Or, 'I saw your guy working at the hardware store', or 'I saw your guy working at the restaurant'."

About mentoring on finances and business help, "You know who retires here, executives and such from all over the country. You call up the retired executives corp around here, and I've had vice-presidents of GM, Young and Rubicon, and others."

On wages, "I'm fairly aware of other organizations kind of like ours in Tempe and Tucson, and I know we're way ahead of them on wages for staff. And people stay here. Ron Aquilera is in his 9th year, Linda Smith 22 years, Rob Colcord 19 years, Esly Isidora Pereya 14, John Ballard 14."

He says having a clear mission statement is very important. In addition, even though they are good friends outside of work, "The job descriptions are the job descriptions, and the evaluation of you is on meeting that description. A tight job description, clear expectations, here's the mission, here's your contribution to the mission, here's what's in it for you, results in a happy workplace. No dead weight here." He adds, "It's a doable mission. That's part of the happy workplace and longevity."

On the work atmosphere and the willingness of local students to take jobs there, "We're a great place for college students to work. We love the Prescott College students, we love the Yavapai College students who we're almost right next door to."

About pitching their services, "I went to Stafford to talk to a parent group and someone asked me if companies actually pay YEI! to have our people do their work, their assembly, their mailings. And I said yeah, they want us to do this work. They want this stuff out of their shop. This is an easy sell to these companies. And as far as getting donations, I don't go out with sack cloth and ashes and guilt trips. I ask, do you want the guy home collecting supplemental security income and watching TV, or do you want him to be able to say, 'I'm a Production

Technician, and I pay my taxes, and I buy stuff at the stores just like everyone else, and I'm just a regular guy'? What do they want? Democrats love it. Republicans love it. And it's my job to present it."

About owning the building, "Why I wanted to own our building outright is so even if a time came when we couldn't pay the light bill, at least we wouldn't have a landlord who could kick us out."

About the possibility of retiring, "I kind of think they're going to haul me out of here feet first. What else am I going to do? And I'm having a ball. I like it."

Kathleen

Kathleen is still running YBBBS. The BBBS agencies in several major cities have approached her over the years wanting her to move to their cities and run their agencies. The national organization also approached her at one time. She is developing a succession plan so that when things are ready she can move on to her next step. When she retires from YBBBS she wants to turn her attention to a mentoring institute, to help expand the science behind mentoring, and to disseminate what is known so it gets used.

One principle of Kathleen's approach to a service agency is how you look at the money: "You never see how much money you could raise and then see how many kids you could serve. Instead you look at how many kids there are, you set a goal for what percentage of the at-risk population you want to serve, and then that is the first building block of your strategic plan. It sort of flips it around."

On working with some of the other five: "We worked closely with the Guidance Clinic and Max Bell to identify kids. Then we worked with Gordon Glau to expand funds from the state because the outcomes were so strong on kids in our program. And he fought, a lot, to keep that money coming and targeted to matching kids. Sometimes there were strings attached to that money that were just unworkable and he would help with that. He was very helpful in getting the state Supreme Court to identify BBBS as a juvenile delinquency prevention organization. It had been recognized that way nationally but in the state it had not. He worked hard to get that recognition.

That's why we started doing statistics on how well our kids were doing. He was much more visionary and much more willing to put his neck on the line to make things happen than many people were willing to do."

On growing: "The thing that happens is you hit a plateau and then you have to change the way you're doing business. The board has to change, the CEO has to change, and the staff has to change. Each one of those factors plateaus. I think you literally have to change every seven years. Either you leave and somebody else comes in, or the board of directors and the CEO have to change in order to reinvent the organization. Because there's a big difference between an organization that has a budget of $250,000 and an organization that has a budget of $1,000,000. What happens is with a lot of agencies they just don't do that. They just keep doing things the same way."

About changes in the culture over the years: "It has been interesting, the sociological changes in the culture that affect the organization. At one time it was very difficult to match gays. Part of the problem was parents weren't willing to accept that. Our point always was that it's not up to us to decide what the moral values of a family should be, it's up to the parents. Our job is to match their moral value system. Whatever they believe is right we should be able to match that. Then there was a huge blow up about that with the Focus on the Family organization who made statements about our organization that weren't true. They said we were matching kids to gays without telling the parents, which wasn't true. Anymore than we would match a Catholic or a Jehovah's Witness, or a person living with another person, or a smoker, or any of the other hot buttons that people have, without that being what the parent wants."

About the struggle to find enough men to be Bigs: "It's always easier to match women. Some years the nationwide number of men coming into the program to be Bigs was only a third of the total. One of the things we did was an aggressive attitude that you have to have one half your matches be boys, and the vast majority of the boys had to be matched to men or families, not to women, which was happening around the country."

Constantly in need of more Bigs, especially men, they regularly try to generate public awareness of the need. One avenue that has helped since 1991 has been the local news paper, the Daily Courier, running an article every week, first called Friday's Child, and later Child of the Week.

An innovation in the program around the country is school based matches, where all of the connection between the Big and Little occurs in school. "National started to go toward school based programs, which I thought were a great idea, but then it became easier. People were getting awards for matching huge numbers of kids but these matches were only lasting months instead of years. So it was always a matter of trying to hold the line, that, yes, high school programs are good, but they have their limitations. So you don't want all your matches being school based, just as you don't want too many of your boys matched with women Bigs, or other standards we wanted to hold, so that you were always looking at measuring lots of different things. What began to happen at national was they began to measure only one thing and that was how many matches. They stopped looking at anything else and it drove all the organizations in the wrong direction. So we had to pull back and we did that well ahead of the National organization because we're based on social science. We've always looked at the numbers."

About careful management of money: "I never had a business class but my parents taught me about money, so I was taught to be fiscally very conservative. Any windfall money, where somebody passed away or gave a large donation of stock, were always put away. They weren't used. Only the interest was used."

That pattern of saving up funds over thirty years was a life saver to them after the economic crash of 2008 and an extreme drop in the donations they received over the next several years. The reserves were important, but so was what the board chose to do with it. Not just use it and hope it lasted long enough to tide them over, but invest it in reorganization and hiring expertise so they could adapt to surviving in a changed economic environment. "So we had all that reserve we had built up over decades to use in bad times, especially this current recession. And even then we didn't just use up the money. We completely turned our ship in another direction. We started doing things we'd never done before. We hired a consultant who had run one of the most successful state agencies and reorganized not only the way we did business but where the money was coming from, and how we used the assets of our staff in a completely different way. I think that foresight helped to create a much better organization."

They did have to make cuts: "We cut out middle management. We didn't cut program staff because that seemed to be the mistake that a lot of people make, in both corporations and non-profit. You look around at schools and it's not the principals who are going. They're not using one principal for two schools. They get rid of teachers. Our theory was that is the last thing you ever want to get rid of are the teachers."

On innovating but being sure it works: "We've always been very innovative. When the high school program came around we were one of the first to do it. We were one of the first to do the school based program. But we never let them take over the organization. And we always watched to see what the outcomes would be."

"The high school program is wonderful because it gives students their first opportunity to volunteer, and it gets children involved in the program that we otherwise would never get access to. So it has a wonderful value. On the other hand it's not complete. Many of the kids end up needing more than just the high school match. But the high school matches are great way to start out. And some of those high school kids become great long time mentors. With the school based program we realized the outcomes weren't very good, they didn't last long, and the research on them from Harvard didn't show any outcomes. But school based where they saw the kids outside the school made a huge difference. So we changed how we did business and we set our strategic plan so that it measured the outcomes we needed."

"But those outcomes had to be multi-faceted in order to have the kind of outcomes we wanted. So on the one hand the board set high goals for us, requiring us to match high numbers of kids, to be responsible and say we're going to match 20 percent of the at-risk kids in the community, even though nationally they're only serving three to five percent. But on the other hand we said we have to have all these other measures. You have to have half the kids be boys, the vast majority matched to men, and make sure matches are lasting a certain amount of time. You have to make sure that your match support is at a very high level of follow up because you want to take care of those matches, and otherwise you don't know when matches are closing and that can skew your data. You want to be sure your Match Advisers are doing good quality work, that they're going in at an early point when a match is having problems, not waiting till it's falling apart. They have to do six-month and one-year in-person evaluations. That you're moving your school based matches into the more effective school based plus program, that you're matching enough minority kids."

On adapting to changing demographics: "One of the things we noticed was that we're in an aging population, but the National organization is still looking for 20 and 30 year olds to be Bigs. We looked at the data and saw that nationally only four percent of the male Bigs are over 50. That doesn't make sense with our aging population. And these are people who have time, because they've raised their kids. Then we looked locally and it was 11 percent of our male Bigs were over 50, even though we had a population of 34 percent over that age. Our feeling was that because of what's going on in people's lives in their 50s, 60s and 70s it should be higher proportionately. So we changed the way we sought out male Bigs. That was what Duane Groce taught us." Duane is a local business man. "He said you need a program for grandfathers. Instead of saying, well we have one, we listened and realized that men saw BBBS as a program for young people. Women didn't care as much, but older men wouldn't come in to be Bigs. We were always looking. I call it good social science."

About paying attention to the numbers: "John Harris (who did the research with Harvard) says we're one of the best mentoring organizations in the country. And he says it's because we look at research, we look at what's really happening. We do an audit. Hardly anybody in the country does an audit other than their financial books. They don't audit they're program. Every year we do a program audit, we bring in outside auditors, we pull files, they do a check to make sure everything we say we do, we do. Why do people have social service programs and they never audit their programs, or only do audits by staff? They only audit their financials? That's not their mission. Their mission isn't money."

"That's one of the things were learned from other high quality organizations. We learned that from another BBBS agency that was doing that and we brought it in. We learned from another agency to hold Match Advisers accountable for their work, that somebody oversaw them. That each Match Adviser has a supervisor who oversaw the work that they were doing and asked about every match and made sure they were doing the work they said they were doing. When we went out and talked about that people said that's a slap in the face of the Match Advisers. You're saying you don't trust them. And our point was, no, they have a very hard job and they need people who can help them be successful. Because some people do a great job but if you don't have somebody reminding you what the priorities are and paying attention to what you're doing, you don't always know what to do, and some people need guidance and support."

"We learned from good agencies all over. Some from the agency in Kansas especially about quality programs. We learned the best ways to do the Bowl-for-Kids-Sake fund raisers from Tucson, Kansas, and Canada. We learned about auditing from Oklahoma. From Bozeman, Montana we learned an approach to make our Dinner and Auction more successful. We recently looked at what Kansas City was doing because they were recruiting more men than women, so we changed our message and the way we were spending our recruitment dollars, and how we were tracking things. Through the National organization we also had access to experts in many fields from molestation prevention, to major giving and planned giving, and we made use of those."

Although she has learned to always verify these innovations: "You hear some agency is doing something, but what I learned a long time ago is that doesn't mean anything. Then you have to go look at the data to see if it bears out. People who do good at business, they're interested, it's part of what drives them and I think it's the same for me. I always want to figure out a way to do it better."

About whether the interest in tracking results came naturally and led to her interest in social science, or the training in social science came first. "Yes. Both. If I think about the things I loved and hated in school, I hated spelling because it was illogical, never made any sense. I loved things like, biology and I had a wonderful biology teacher. I had a great history teacher in high school who talked about how social systems and the way people thought affected outcomes dramatically. I had a wonderful education in my high school years that was geared toward college, being taught to work hard, to think outside the box, and the Jesuits rule that if you can't argue both side of a question you don't have an opinion, you have someone else's. I think that had a lot to do with it."

"When I went to college I had great sociology teachers. I had a teacher name Dr. Nagaswa, who, in the 60s, brought in a prostitute to talk to us, someone from the John Birch Society, a professional boxer who was gay. You were literally not being told how to think, but you were being given information and challenged, okay, think about this. And a great sociology statistics teacher, Dr. Lindbergh who taught how to look at data and how to prove or disprove and not cheat. And there was a wonderful teacher in the social work department who taught the other side of it, how do you work with people. How do you help people without enabling them. How do you support them. How do you get the most out of somebody. If you're real black-and-white and have a dogma about how people are supposed to be you can't help somebody be a successful Big because each one brings strengths and weaknesses and your job is to figure out how to bring out their strengths, help them be the most successful Big they can be."

How some of her current and recent board members helped, and how the diversity of skills helped. "I think of people like Martin Gottlieb, who said, 'You're good but you're not excellent'. That type of push. It's partly my nature, but it's partly using the tremendous skill sets of our board of directors. And that's one of the biggest draw backs many agencies have. They don't use their board members. They try to control their board members or just keep them on the sidelines. You have to be willing to be held accountable, heavily accountable. It's a lot harder to have a powerful board because they're the ones that are holding you accountable. A lot of people don't want to do that. The board is also responsible for choosing new board members. We say here's what we want, here's the skill sets we need at this time on this board, which might be different than what we needed five years ago or five years from now. Then we evaluate the current board's skills and look for people who can fill in the missing skill sets."

"This happened when we needed to build our building because of growing staff. We needed different kinds of people on the board than we did when the board only needed to focus on fund raising for programs. Now our board probably needs a lot of breadth because you need people who are good at developing the Bowl for Kids Sake fund raiser and making connections there, but you also need people who have the kind of connections with individuals who are willing to give to help kids. At the same time you need some business people who can look at how we can diversify our funding. It takes a lot of different skill sets."

"We're are developing planned giving, a lot more endowment. You need a board member who understands that, who's legally capable of setting up a 501(c)3 or making a decision about whether that's a good or bad idea. Paul Border has tremendous skills in this area and is working on that. Perry Massie, the current board chair, has encouraged us to set bold goals, and, as with others, has been very generous himself. Travis Rushing was tremendously important to us because he took us through a real strategic planning, where we had a plan that we used every single day that was driven by measures and every measure had to have numbers, and every goal had to have a measure and an outcome. Martin Gottlieb took us from being a small board of a bunch of nice people into a much more highly successful board. Harold Greenberg required us to evaluate our business practices. Anna Young has done a great job with our program audit. Carol Clayton has been a gentle warrior, never letting us forget our mission. Each of these board chairs, and other members of the board, brings a strength to the organization that we wouldn't have otherwise. Don Hecht has been on our board and a major donor, and important over the last few challenging years in encouraging us to remember to keep children first."

"It's important having great people involved, because hardly anybody else did what we did, when we took an incredibly aggressive attitude toward surviving the downturn. The board did that. I don't know that I would have ever done it without such a strong and involved board. I suppose what I bring to it is the willingness to change, the willingness to stick my neck out. When everybody else was pulling in they said, 'We're hiring a consultant and we're going to do it a different way.' And they spent money to do that. Most people would have said that was the wrong thing to do. It's about the ability to bring together the right people."

"My part is that people have to believe in me. They have to believe that I'm going to try to do the best thing. It doesn't mean I'm always going to do the right thing but hopefully I can be altruistic enough that my ego and my fear doesn't get in the way of the organization. So you spend two years of not sleeping well at night, and being really scared whether the changes will work, and you have to be willing to do that. And if you're not willing to do that then you need to get out of the way and let someone else take over. That's what you see often in non-profits. They're good people, they care about the organization, and nobody wants to fire them, but they're holding the organization back."

"And if you run a non-profit you have a much higher need for that accountability. If you run a business and your business is to make money for the owner, that's what your business is. You may not care whether the owner makes more money. You may figure you're working hard enough. But when you do *this* kind of work it's very different because the organization belongs to these children whose lives are affected by your choices. And if you make bad choices they go to prison, they get pregnant, they never finish high school. And so I think it's much more critical than how much money you can make, or how much money your stock holders make."

About not getting stuck when it's time to grow to the next level: "You see it in non-profits because they want to find some other reason when things don't work. You see it in how different agencies handle the Bowl-for-Kids-Sake fund raiser. 'Well Bowl-for-Kids-Sake is passe, you can't make as much money as you used to.' Yes you can, but you have to do some really hard work to do it, and you have to change and you have to grow and do things differently. Gordon's operation grew enormously and he was considered one of the best in the state because he never lost site of his mission, he never lost site of who his client was. He was incredible that way. He always did what was best for those kids, and he remembered they were children and didn't let the politics of the day affect him, like some other people do."

About how the agency overlapped with the other five, in addition to the work she did with Gordon: "The Guidance Clinic, in the early years, housed us, and Don was on the board of directors. We serviced some of Max's kids from CPS. We worked some of the same population as John at Catholic Social Services. We referred people to CSS for help. Brad is a Big Brother. On occasion we would service one of his clients, and he was always generous in things like letting us borrow one of his vans to haul our kids to and event."

"With Judge Brutinel, he started these great drug programs which were a help to some of our parents who needed to go through them. He was always highly supportive because he knew ours was a program that kept kids out of the courts. He was always willing to try to help one of our kids if we had a special issue. Our job was to try to match with Bigs the kids that were being referred into the court system, early, and keep them out of the system. They got arrested but maybe went into a diversion program and we would match those kids with Bigs so they wouldn't end up staying in the system. We took them at the earliest point in order to decrease recidivism and that's what the statistics show, that our kids are half as likely to be arrested as all other kids in the community. So we're taking high risk kids and they're doing better than all other kids in the community."

About Prescott: "Prescott is our home base but we work in eighteen communities around the county. We probably have as many matches in Prescott Valley as in Prescott. But that wasn't always true. When we first started we served Prescott more heavily than anybody else because that's where the population was."

"I guess you would say that Prescott was the power behind YBBBS. And that power affected the whole county. We're serving eighteen communities and sixty one schools, the schools that have ninety percent of the kids in Yavapai County. I think the sense of Prescott as a community has allowed that to happen. People move here because they want to be part of a community. They seem to be more community oriented than maybe somewhere else. I think that has had a positive affect on the organization. Prescott is the power in the sense that most of the board members come from here, the majority of the money comes from here. Not all. Prescott Valley continues to grow in influence. We have some very good people in the Verde. But we have relied on the Prescott area to keep it going. So that sense of community and where people know each other and work together on things has had a positive effect."

"On the other hand the city of Prescott doesn't give anybody money for anything. Unlike Sedona and Chino Valley and lots of places across the country that have city money to help support. They don't see it in any way as their responsibility. I think, personally, that that's financially foolish. It's not about responsibility, it's about fiscal responsibility. If you can spend a thousand dollars on a preventative program like BBBS and save ten to twenty thousand dollars on kids not ending up in trouble you should be doing that. Kids who end up in legal trouble in the juvenile system cost $60,000 a year on average."

"It's good for the economy to spend some preventative money up front. I think that's one of the problems, we don't see that if we put more money into this, and required it to be well run—because I think there are mentoring organizations you can put money into and it won't do you any good—but if you can do that and save the taxpayers money, then I think you should be held responsible for doing that. People will say you can't help everybody. No, you can't. But if there's an organization that can prove with research that by spending your money, as Scott Mabery (who took over Juvenile Probation after Gordon) said, 'If I could take all the money I spend incarcerating kids and spend it on mentoring I would.' Because he'd get a better outcome for the money. But he can't. The city could do more of that sort of thing that would help to relieve the city coffers. They would have more money. But that's not what ends up happening. We build jails rather than spending money on prevention."

"There's a great sense of community in Prescott and people are willing. Not everybody. There are a lot of people who come here and don't even want to support the schools. They come here to live a good life where they are safe and happy. They don't want to be bothered and feel they've already paid their way. But I think a lot of people come here because they have a sense of community. There are a lot of people who come here and retire early and they are very generous people. So that helps. If it was a poor community it would be harder to raise major money."

Advice for those who follow: "I guess the sage advice is accountability. The other piece is to remember to whom the organization belongs. It belongs to the children, it doesn't belong to the staff. It's hard in this business; you have good people who work hard, they're good people, but their presence on your staff will limit the services to children. That's probably one of the hardest parts, because people don't do this to make money, they do this because they care, but sometimes they don't have the right skill sets, and people too often take care of their staff and not the children."

"But the other is accountability, holding yourself accountable, that you are going to be your own worst enemy. Because it's so easy for it to get comfortable and your faults will affect the success of the organization, your weaknesses, your blind points, whatever it is, they are the things that will have a negative effect. And it will be exacerbated more so than anybody else's weak points because you're at the top of the organization."

"The other thing is don't reinvent the wheel. There are people out there who know how to do things really well. Go find out how to do it and bring that into the organization. But make sure that you research it well and that it's based on fact, not on some flowery speech that somebody gives."

"And remember to stay on your mission. Mentoring is what we do. We don't do everything else. We do mentoring."

"But it gets back to being accountable."

About a future mentoring institute: "To me the saddest part of this work is you have all this knowledge, and how do you make it accessible to others? And how do you also test, have a place where you can really test outcomes instead of it taking years for things, because you're always running as fast as you can run, and you don't have time, sometimes, to evaluate whether something is valuable or not valuable?"

"What is needed is a research institute where you could take the best ideas and be able to train other people on how to do that. And to somehow have the National organization use that kind of knowledge to hold the agencies accountable, because they don't. They don't hold us accountable at the level they should. They set minimum standards but they don't hold us accountable enough. How do you create a situation where the people who have knowledge in the field can get that knowledge to the National organization? I'm not sure how you do that but those are the pieces that I would be interested in working on."

"What I've seen is researchers doing fabulous research but then it's never tested in a real environment. We know this or that, and this is what you should do, but they don't ever come and take that great research and then incorporate people like me who do the work and bring those two pieces together. Then you would really have some high quality information. That's what I'd love to see happen."

"I was just talking with a researcher and they know stuff I don't know, but it's very rare that they have the experience of having run a mentoring organization. The sad thing is that those two pieces aren't brought together. People in universities and who have written books on it, but they don't even know what the measurements are to use, to know whether they're getting the kind of outcome they want. They don't know because they aren't there in the day-to-day work. So how would you bring that practical side together with the academic side?"

Which is why she hopes to continue the kind of work they did with Harvard. "We did empirical research with them. They put in place certain questions, certain tools that tested outcomes and we applied those. This was the first time this kind of research was being done and the outcomes studied and applied." Previous research had shown that mentoring works. The Harvard research was digging deeper. Why does it work? What are the steps in the process? What changes does the child go through, like a change in attitude toward school or toward the world? How do you monitor those to see whether that's happening in a given match, or which matches have that and why? What is the relationship between the strength of the bond between the Big and the Little, and the outcome? And how do you monitor that as the match continues over time?

A limiting factor was time. Match Advisers who already had full loads were trying to add documenting and research to their work. For the research to be done right it needs to add staff support to carry that increased load.

"The problem is we were doing it with not enough money. You've got staff who are trying to do program and trying to do research too. It's really hard. It puts tremendous stress on the staff, on the organization in general."

With all of this existing success behind her she nevertheless looks forward. That is exactly why she hopes to be able to form a mentoring institute after retirement from YBBBS, which she would like to do as soon as it is practical. To help BBBS agencies and mentoring programs all over the country who are operating in ways that are known to be less than optimal. To get what is already know better disseminated and used. And to do more of that bringing together of the research on what works, with the practical knowledge of those who are doing the work, so that the next generation can help even more kids. "That is the very kind of thing I would like to do."

EPILOGUE

In retirement Don worked for a while in social services for the Yavapai Indian tribe. Ironically, later John took that same position. In some ways they are still the go-to people in their field.

Don and John, along with Gordon and Max have lunch together regularly. They refer to themselves as the "old geezers" club.

Brad, as he said, expects to keep on until they carry him out feet first, and it is hoped when he is no longer there that YEI will be well structured to continue their wonderful service.

Kathleen hopes to retire when it is possible so that she can create the mentoring institute she talked of, to smooth the way for an even more successful next generation.

INDEX
OF PEOPLE AND PLACES

ABOUT THE AUTHOR

Tom Cantlon is a twenty year resident of the Prescott area. A business owner and author, and writes a column every Wednesday for the local news paper. A book of selected earlier columns up to 2006 is due out in December of 2011. TomCantlon@TomCantlon.com

AGENCY CONTACTS AND DONATIONS

All of the agencies in this story would welcome your help. Some are more dependent on private donations than others. Big Brothers/Big Sisters to a large degree, and Yavapai Exceptional Industries less so, are more dependent than, for instance, Juvenile Probation which is government funded. Even Juvenile Probation, though, welcomes volunteers for programs like its Community Juvenile Justice Court.

Yavapai Big Brothers/Big Sisters
3208 Lakeside Village Dr, Prescott AZ 86301
AZBigs.org   928-778-5135

~

YEI! (Yavapai Exceptional Industries)
436 N Washington Av, Prescott AZ 86301
YEIWorks.com   928-445-0991

~

Catholic Charities
434 W Gurley St, Prescott AZ 86301
CatholicCharitiesAZ.com   928-778-2531

~

West Yavapai Guidance Clinic
642 Dameron Dr, Prescott AZ 86301
WYGC.org   928-445-5211

~

Yavapai Juvenile Probation
960 Division St, Prescott AZ 86301
co.yavapai.az.us/jp.aspx   928-771-3156

~

Child Protective Services
www.azdes.gov/child_protective_services   888-767-2445

Made in the USA
Charleston, SC
01 December 2011